Beyond the Ordinary

HEALTH, WEALTH, & WISDOM
STRATEGIES FOR DYNAMIC LIVING

GENE BAILEY

Unless otherwise noted, Scripture quotations are taken from the New King James Version of the Bible. Copyright © 1979, 1980, 1982 by Thomas Nelson, Inc. Used by permission. All rights reserved.

Scripture quotations marked KJV are taken from The King James Version of the Bible.

Scripture quotations marked NIV are taken from the Holy Bible, New International Version.® NIV®. Copyright © 1973, 1978, 1984, by International Bible Society. Used by permission of Zondervan Publishing House. All rights reserved.

Scripture quotations marked RSV are taken from the Revised Standard Version of the Bible. Copyright © 1946, Old Testament section copyright © 1952 by the Division of Christian Education of the Churches of Christ in the United States of America and is used by permission.

Beyond The Ordinary
Health, Wealth, and Wisdom Strategies for Dynamic Living
Copyright © 2008 by Gene Bailey
All rights reserved.

Written permission must be secured from the publisher to use or reproduce any part of this book, except for brief quotations in critical reviews or articles.

Gene Bailey
1450 Hughes Road
Suite 110
Grapevine, TX 76051

ISBN: 978-0-615-22226-4
Printed in the United States of America.

Table of Contents

Introduction

Section 1 - Health

Chapter 1	Body, Soul & Spirit - The Total Picture	8
Chapter 2	What's Holding You Back?	19
Chapter 3	Your Total Wellness Plan	37

Section 2 - Wealth

Chapter 4	True Riches	66
Chapter 5	Time - Our Most Valuable Asset	86
Chapter 6	Positioning Yourself For Success	101

Section 3 - Wisdom

Chapter 7	The Beginning of Wisdom	121
Chapter 8	How Hungry Are You?	135
Chapter 9	Living Your Life Right Now	157

A Final Word

Introduction

Do you dream about your destiny, or are you living it? Beyond the ordinary is where everybody wants to live; yet, most people don't know how to get there!

I've got good news for you! It's never too late to start!

For example, the name Harland Sanders may have little or no meaning to you, yet when you say Colonel Sanders, that's a different story, for people all over the world have enjoyed the "finger lickin' good chicken" of this restaurant entrepreneur and pioneer of fast food. Colonel Sanders' story wasn't always one of success. His challenges began at age six when his father died. To support the family his mother peeled tomatoes in a canning factory in the daytime, and earned extra money by sewing at night. At the young age of six Sanders learned to cook so he could take care of his siblings. He got his first job at the age of ten, working on a nearby farm. He dropped out of school in the seventh grade, and worked various jobs during his teen years, including steamboat driver, streetcar conductor, insurance salesman, farmer, railroad firefighter, and eventually enlisted in the Army. He even earned a law degree by taking a correspondence course.

By age 40 he had a service station in Corbin, Kentucky, located on U.S. Route 25 at the edge of the Appalachian Mountains. Travelers stopping at the service station began to inquire where they could get something to eat, so Sanders began serving food to his customers in his living quarters. This expanded to a motel and a restaurant with seating for 142 people. Sanders focused on the cooking, perfecting his method of cooking chicken. He focused the seasonings, altering his chicken recipe until it was "just right". He also used a modified pressure cooker that allowed him to cook the chicken faster, allowing him to serve more customers. Sanders discovered that chicken cooked in this unconventional way was much more moist and flavorful, and quickly became a favorite for his customers.

World War II gas rationing discouraged travel and in 1956 a new highway was built, bypassing Sander's restaurant in Corbin. This drastically affected his business, and before long he was forced to auction off the property just to pay his bills. At age 66 Sanders was almost broke, living off his monthly Social Security check of $105. Many thought he was washed up because he was too old and had failed so many times.

But "the Colonel" wasn't ready to give up yet! With nothing to lose, he packed up his secret recipe of 11 spices and his pressure cooker, and began visiting restaurant owners in attempt to convince them to use his recipe in exchange for royalties for each chicken dish sold. He was rejected over 3,000 times before he made his first sale! He signed up restaurant owners, an early form of franchising, shipping them his secret recipe seasoning, if they agreed to pay him five cents for every chicken dinner served.

This is how he got started. The number of franchises continued to grow, expanding to thousands of locations in the U.S. and overseas.

This is the story of ONE man ... ONE man that was considered too old, washed up, a failure at everything he did. But one day when he received his monthly Social Security check of $105, something changed within him. Even though he was still unemployed, living on a meager retirement check of $105 a month, he decided to do something about it! He said no to the status quo! And when he did, his dreams blossomed into his destiny!

Sometimes it takes a "bad-things-happen-to-good-people" kind of experience to push them into their destiny. It certainly did for Harland Sanders. And the fact you are reading this book says one thing: you're ready to say goodbye to the ordinary. You are ready to do whatever it takes to get to your divine appointed place in life and experience dynamic living. Regardless of circumstances or what people have said about you, despite mistakes you may have made or any other negative thing that has happened in your life to keep you down, you're not going to settle for ordinary any longer!

Look at what happened when ONE man refused to let the world get him down. What will happen with YOU when you realize the future is ripe with opportunity in your life? Beginning right now, start living *beyond the ordinary*!

Section 1

Health

Pronunciation: `'helth also heltth`
Function: *noun*
Usage: often attributive
Etymology: Middle English *helthe*, from Old English h[AE]lth, from hAl

1. a: the condition of being sound in body, mind, or spirit; *especially* : freedom from physical disease or pain b : the general condition of the body <in poor *health*> <enjoys good *health*>
2. a : flourishing condition : *well being* b : general condition or state <poor economic *health*>
3. a toast to someone's health or prosperity[1]

Chapter One
Body, Soul, and Spirit - The Total Picture

We grow great by dreams. All big men are dreamers. They see things in the soft haze of a spring day or in the red fire of a long winter's evening. Some of us let these great dreams die, but others nourish and protect them; nurse them through bad days till they bring them to the sunshine and light which comes always to those who sincerely hope that their dreams will come true.

Woodrow Wilson
28th US President

Is your life everything you want it to be, or do you long to live an extraordinary life where yesterday's dreams blossom into realities that unlock your destiny? If you feel as if you have been tied to the status quo and your dreams are bigger than the moment you are living in, keep reading!

Beyond the ordinary is where everybody wants to live; yet, most people don't know how to get there. I've got good news for you! You can awaken the dreamer within, say goodbye to the ordinary, and experience dynamic living 24 hours a day —starting today!

I believe this kind of dynamic living is linked to three areas: health, wealth, and wisdom. I want to examine each of these areas, and help you recognize your God-given ambitions and dreams, set up an action plan for reaching your goals, and ultimately focus on becoming all that you are designed to be.

You just read the dictionary definition of health, and I will offer definitions of wealth and wisdom prior to sections two and three.

As with everything in life, however, it is one thing for Noah Webster (or one of his descendants) to tell us what something is, but it's another thing to make it personal. The Bible has quite a bit to say about the subjects. Perhaps the best illustration of health, wealth, and wisdom, especially in the Old Testament, is the not-so-hidden treasure running like rich veins of precious ore throughout the story of Joseph.

THE DREAMER

Just in case you're not familiar with the story or you weren't listening during Sunday school, here is the Cliff Notes® version:

- Joseph was Jacob's eleventh child.
- Even as a boy, he had the God-given gift of interpreting dreams.
- He discovered that having dreams that foretell of your brothers and parents kneeling before you doesn't necessarily endear the dream interpreter to his siblings.
- At the age of seventeen, Joseph was a shepherd like his brothers.
- Jacob made a splendid robe for Joseph, often referred

to as the "coat of many colors."
- Joseph was sold into slavery by his brothers—mad with jealousy because they knew that their father loved Joseph more than any of them—and taken by caravan to Egypt.
- Joseph found favor in his new country; his diligence and trustworthiness helped him move from being a slave to a household servant.
- As head of Potiphar's household, Joseph's handsomeness attracted Potiphar's wife, who cried "rape" when Joseph didn't respond to her advances.
- Needless to say, Potiphar had little choice but to cast Joseph in prison for his "wrongdoing."
- In prison, Joseph once again found favor. He interpreted dreams for two of the Pharaoh's assistants.
- As a result, Joseph was eventually called before Pharaoh. After the young Hebrew interpreted a dream that proved important to Egypt's future, he was promoted to the powerful position of Pharaoh's chief assistant.
- After seven years of plenty, seven years of famine began throughout the region—just as Joseph had foretold when asked to interpret Pharaoh's dream.
- The drought brought Joseph's brothers to Egypt seeking grain, and in a twist of historic irony, not only did the brothers bow before their brother, fulfilling the young man's dream, but Joseph also forgave his brothers who had betrayed him and sold him into slavery.

The brothers enjoyed a joyous, tearful reunion, and then went back to Canaan to bring their father to Joseph. The entire family was given land and food in Egypt during the famine and beyond. A dreamer was used to help an entire generation of Egyptians and Jacob's descendants survive a life-threatening disaster.

What would have happened to Egypt and Jacob's family without Joseph, the dreamer, who thrived wherever he was—body, soul and spirit—no matter what challenges he faced? This is a question we should be asking today, for the answer is life changing!

HEALTH, WEALTH, AND WISDOM

Joseph was a dreamer from his youngest years, yet his dreams were fulfilled in remarkable ways. The journey of this dreamer to his extraordinary destiny took him some unexpected places, including a pit, a prison and finally, the palace. Despite the many low moments, his life is the epitome of many ideals, especially in the areas of health, wealth, and wisdom, which are highlighted in this book:

- *Health*

Genesis 39:6 says, *"Now Joseph was handsome in form and appearance."* Somehow, despite the brutality he sometimes faced as a slave, his health thrived. He was certainly attractive to the women of his day, including the Potiphar's wife.

More importantly, his knowledge and understanding of dietary needs and practices helped an entire region of the world survive a devastating famine.

- *Wealth*

Even as a slave in Potiphar's house, the Bible speaks of Joseph prospering:

> *"Now Joseph had been taken down to Egypt. And Potiphar, an officer of Pharaoh, captain of the guard, an Egyptian, bought him from the Ishmaelites who had taken him down there. The Lord was with Joseph, and he was a successful man; and*

> *he was in the house of his master the Egyptian. And his master saw that the Lord was with him and that the Lord made all he did to prosper in his hand. So Joseph found favor in his sight, and served him. Then he made him overseer of his house, and all that he had he put under his authority. So it was, from the time that he had made him overseer of his house and all that he had, that the Lord blessed the Egyptian's house for Joseph's sake; and the blessing of the Lord was on all that he had in the house and in the field."*
>
> Genesis 39:1-5

Potiphar not only saw that Joseph could be trusted, but he also especially understood that Joseph was blessed by God. Even after the horrible turn of events caused by Potiphar's wife, Joseph prospered while in prison.

> *"Then Joseph's master took him and put him into the prison, a place where the king's prisoners were confined. And he was there in the prison. But the Lord was with Joseph and showed him mercy, and He gave him favor in the sight of the keeper of the prison. And the keeper of the prison committed to Joseph's hand all the prisoners who were in the prison; whatever they did there, it was his doing. The keeper of the prison did not look into anything that was under Joseph's authority, because the Lord was with him; and whatever he did, the Lord made it prosper."*
>
> Genesis 39:20-23

Joseph reached a new level of success. He had absolute power over all the prison. Some might call it merely being in the right place at the right time or attribute it to "good luck." The Bible, however, gives credit directly to

the Lord.
- *Wisdom*

Throughout Joseph's life, his wisdom rose above the situations in which he found himself. He was called before the ruler of all Egypt to interpret the Pharaoh's dreams.

> *"So the advice was good in the eyes of Pharaoh and in the eyes of all his servants. And Pharaoh said to his servants, "Can we find such a one as this, a man in whom is the Spirit of God?" Then Pharaoh said to Joseph, "Inasmuch as God has shown you all this, there is no one as discerning and wise as you. You shall be over my house, and all my people shall be ruled according to your word; only in regard to the throne will I be greater than you." And Pharaoh said to Joseph, "See, I have set you over all the land of Egypt." Then Pharaoh took his signet ring off his hand and put it on Joseph's hand; and he clothed him in garments of fine linen and put a gold chain around his neck. And he had him ride in the second chariot which he had; and they cried out before him, "Bow the knee!" So he set him over all the land of Egypt. Pharaoh also said to Joseph, "I am Pharaoh, and without your consent no man may lift his hand or foot in all the land of Egypt." And Pharaoh called Joseph's name Zaphnath-Paaneah. And he gave him as a wife Asenath, the daughter of Poti-Pherah priest of On. So Joseph went out over all the land of Egypt. Joseph was thirty years old when he stood before Pharaoh king of Egypt. And Joseph went out from the presence of Pharaoh, and went throughout all the land of Egypt".*
>
> Genesis 41:37-46

Says Bible scholar Finis Dake:

> *"Joseph spoke by inspiration and faith, remembering the dreams he had told his brethren. He felt that God had already made clear a great destiny for him. This consciousness of God's will made him speak with freedom and authority to recommend the line of action for Pharaoh that would save the nation, and especially his own people, from famine. Pharaoh was prepared, by the startling and vivid revelation of God to him, to hear and adopt Joseph's plan."*[2]

So much had been crammed into Joseph's first thirty years, yet as he passed test after test, this godly man of health, wealth, and wisdom was divinely blessed and inspired by Jehovah.

A DREAMER'S TESTIMONY OF HEALTH, WEALTH, AND WISDOM

Joseph was a youthful dreamer whose dreams were fulfilled (Genesis 41:42-44). He was faithful in the hardest of places and challenges (Genesis 39:1-6; 20-23). He was strong enough to resist the greatest pressure and temptation (Genesis 39:7-13). He was balanced and wise enough to not be overwhelmed by sudden prosperity (Genesis 41:14-46). He was known at home and abroad for his dependence on and faith in God (Genesis 41:16; 45:8). In the end, despite a lifetime of hurts, potential disillusionment, and disappointments, he forgave those who hurt him the worst (Genesis 50:15-21).

Quoting again from Dakes: *"What a generous forgiveness of his brethren; what a comfort to those who had sinned; and what a faith in God to see His hand in 22 long years of homesickness, insulting accusations, physical torment, and mental cruelty!"*[3]

Joseph's amazing testimony of health, wealth, and wisdom became a lasting witness. Years after his death, his children were still receiving an inheritance due to his legacy. In Joshua 24:32 we read:

"The bones of Joseph, which the children of Israel had brought up out of Egypt, they buried at Shechem, in the plot of ground which Jacob had bought from the sons of Hamor the father of Shechem for one hundred pieces of silver, and which had become an inheritance of the children of Joseph."

In a final note on Joseph's life, his reference to El-Shaddai (Genesis 43:14—translated God Almighty in English) is certainly no accident. El-Shaddai means "all-bountiful, the Supplier of all things." Joseph obviously knew who his Supplier was. It is a lesson we must learn, as well, if we are to move into a life of divine health, wealth, and wisdom.

Throughout the Bible, the use of the name El-Shaddai emphasizes the providence of God over all creation, as Joseph obviously knew.

El-Shaddai brings health and healing (Exodus 15:26; Psalm 91; 103:3-5; Isaiah 53:3-5; 1 Peter 2:24; 3 John 2).
- El-Shaddai gives wealth (1 Samuel 2:7-8; 1 Kings 2:3-4; Psalm 1:1-3; Matthew 7:7-11; John 14:12-15; 2 Corinthians 9:6-8; 3 John 2).
- El-Shaddai pours wisdom and understanding on His children, beginning with salvation (Psalm 50:23; Romans 10:9-10; Hebrews 7:25), for God alone fulfills all our greatest needs of body, mind, and spirit (Mark 11:22-24; John 15:7; John 16:23; James1:4-8; Hebrews 11:6).

Health, wealth, and wisdom, both then and now, come from one Source—God Almighty! Health, wealth, and wisdom are fueled by our God-given dreams.

A FINAL NOTE

What will you do with the dreams placed deep inside of you? What steps are you willing to take to encourage your body, soul, and spirit to move into a new, balanced life of health, wealth, and wisdom? What can you do today to go beyond the ordinary and discover your destiny?

I included the story of Colonel Harlan Sanders in the introduction, and spotlighted the story Joseph in this chapter for one reason: both are powerful dreamers.

I believe there's a dreamer in each of us, and in many ways, this is a book for and about dreamers. It provides a common thread, a workable system, for those dreamers who are unwilling to accept the status quo as the basis for life. It is for those who refuse to accept the limitations of the past and present as they build a better tomorrow. It is also for would-be dreamers who are struggling to unshackle themselves from boring, dull lives.

Beyond The Ordinary is expressly devoted to people who desire to make a difference in life—personally, emotionally, spiritually, and professionally. It is offered to help transform a reactive, unhealthy mind set into a creative, ground-breaking attitude to turn your God-given dreams into your destiny.

My desire for you is that you become a you-changer; then a world-changer. As you develop the creativity, persistence, and determination needed to become a you-changer, you will also be well on your way to becoming a world-class dreamer and doer.

From this point on, we will focus on the "little" things in life that don't always seem so important; yet once you make these positive choices—body, soul, and spirit—you will never want to go back to the way you used to be.
Before we go any farther, however, let's find out what has been holding you back.

Personal Health, Wealth, and Wisdom Insight

One key to a life of health, wealth, and wisdom is finding ways to be more aware of your deepest attitudes and beliefs. Locate a notebook right now, and jot down a few thoughts about each of the following questions. I suggest that you keep it nearby as you read this book for use in future exercises as well.

1. List the following, from most important to least important, in terms of where your life is right now:
    Friends
    Family
    Career
    Spiritual growth
    Fitness
    Politics
    Community involvement
    Academic pursuits
    Personal achievement

2. What does the order of the above say about where you are right now—physically, emotionally, and spiritually?

3. What would be the ideal order for your list?

4. What are the three most fulfilling or significant experiences of your life thus far?

5. What are three of your current yet unfulfilled dreams?

6. How are those three dreams different from your goals five years ago?

Chapter One Highlights

- The Bible has quite a bit to say about the subjects of health, wealth, and wisdom. Perhaps the best illustration is the story of Joseph.

- What would have happened to Egypt as well as his family without Joseph, the dreamer, who thrived—body, soul, and spirit—no matter what challenges he faced? It is a question we should be asking today. The answers are life changing.

- What will you do with the dreams placed deep inside of you? What will you do to allow and encourage your body, soul, and spirit to move into a new, harmonious, abundant life of health, wealth, and wisdom?

To be a dreamer is to be misunderstood. Beware when the great God lets loose a thinker on this planet. Then all things are at risk.[4]

Ralph Waldo Emerson

Chapter Two
What's Holding You Back?

Take a moment to think about what you would do if you were given a brand-new body right now. Chances are, you would have no conscious choice but to hold yourself within your 'new' body exactly as you had held yourself within your 'old' body. You would probably impose all the old habits, tensions, and imbalances immediately on your new body because you have come to develop a psychosomatic self-image that surrounds you as tightly as does your skin. The only way you could do anything different with your 'new' body would be if you somehow were also able to assume a 'new' way of being in this body. This new awareness, this changed self-image, comes only with an alteration in being, feeling, thinking, and believing. So, then, it would seem that unless there is a corresponding change in the habits and attitudes that create the body shape, purely physical manipulations of the body are left without a new mental structure in which to take root.[5]

Ken Dychtwald

You—no matter where you are or what you are doing with your life—are an amazing creation. You are the product of an incredibly complex design. Even a cursory glance tells you that any human—composed of mind, body, and spirit—form a magnificent organism capable of achieving almost unbelievable feats.

It is no wonder that King David wrote, *"I will praise You, for I am fearfully and wonderfully made; marvelous are Your works, and that my soul knows very well"* (Psalm 139:14).

The body's entire structure, from head to foot, is a miracle of precision engineering and production. The major organs alone, all ten of them, perform such unique feats of electric conduction that it takes volumes to explain each one adequately.

If you are an adult of average weight, the following list of achievements is only a small part of what your body accomplishes every day:

- Your heart beats over 100,000 times.
- Your blood travels over 150 million miles.
- You breathe over 23,000 times.
- You inhale 438 cubic feet of air.
- You eat over 3 pounds of food.
- You drink nearly 3 quarts of liquids.
- You speak nearly 30,000 words.
- You move specific muscles 750 times.
- You exercise seven million brain cells.
- There are at least several trillion hardworking cells inside you, each so small that it takes 250 of them, placed side by side, to equal the size of a small speck.
- Your inner ear can detect 15,000 different tones, as well as controlling your equilibrium.
- Even though your brain will forget more than 90 per-

cent of what you learn during your lifetime, it will still store 10 times more information than in the 20 million volumes within the Library of Congress.
- Your heart beats an average of 75 times a minute, 40 million times a year—nearly 3 billion times in your lifetime.
- Your heart pumps nearly 3,000 gallons of blood a day, nearly 650,000 gallons a year—more than enough to fill 80 gasoline tank trucks.

The most extraordinary part is how well your body, mind, and spirit are designed to work together in perfect harmony. Ideally.

Unfortunately, we don't always live in an ideal world.

WHAT'S HOLDING YOU BACK?

What is keeping you from achieving your dream of an abundant life of health, wealth, and wisdom?

Charles

Perhaps you are like a man named Charles[6] who at 43 years of age had a Ph.D. in chemical engineering, was a highly paid corporate executive for a large biomedical company, yet had reached a mind-numbing level of career burnout. He began having numerous physical ailments, and doctors didn't seem to be able to help. Physical therapy and deep-tissue bodywork helped some, but didn't resolve all the problems.

As he went through the bodywork sessions, Charles began going through some of the painful feelings that were associated with his past choices. As he got more in tune with his feelings and emotions, he was able to "let go" of the trauma associated with his memories. He started seeing a Christian counselor, which also helped unearth past emotions. Finally he was able to share his feelings of grief—the result of the choices he had made—with his wife and pastor. By fully experiencing and acknowledging the feelings associated with his choices, he became increasingly free of the emotional prison, which he had allowed to hold him captive.

Thankfully, his wife was very supportive through this entire process. As he became more and more aware how closely connected his body, emotions, and spirit were, he also became increasingly aware that many of his physical traumas and the career burnout were closely related to the unshakable fact that he wasn't happy with the decisions that he had simply learned to live with.

"When I was young," Charles said, "I always wanted to be a youth worker, a high school teacher or maybe even a coach. Truth is, part of the way through college, I made a decision that I wanted a career that would make a lot of money. While my own family was always caught in some kind of financial instability, I wanted something different, no matter what it cost. There were a lot of other things and people that influenced my decision, but I was the one who ultimately made that choice to pursue money and stability. Even as I climbed the ladder of success, there was always that nagging feeling that I wasn't doing what I had been destined to do. Frankly, I got locked into a life that I really didn't want. Even when I thought about changing careers and simplifying my life, there was too much riding on my shoulders—my wife, my kids, mortgages, the vacation home, others on the team, my social responsibilities—to even think of doing something different."

When he was forced by all the physical problems to finally take stock of his life, Charles made another set of choices.

"Thankfully, I had reached a level of financial success

so I could check out other options," he shared. "In the end, I eased my way out of the corporate world, even as everyone thought I had completely gone crazy, then began volunteering as an assistant coach at a small Christian school near our home. That was four years ago. I'm now coaching and teaching full time at the same school, and loving every minute of it. Sure, my old cohorts in the corporate world still ask when I'm getting back in the 'real world,' but I just smile and tell them I'm already there. And you know the best part; I'm better physically than I've ever been. Most of the ailments I had are gone...well, except sore muscles every now and then when I try to act like I'm still a teenager on the football field."

Today the knee problems have been alleviated. The chronic throb in his back and shoulder are gone. He is now realizing a level of leadership, physical activity, communication, and well-being that had previously eluded him.

Disguises

Said Francois, Duc de La Rochefoucauld, the classical French author and philosopher, "We are so accustomed to wearing a disguise before others that eventually we are unable to recognize ourselves."

As I travel throughout the world in my speaking and consulting work, I never cease to be surprised at the great number of people who have become extraordinary wearers of disguises, even as they riddle themselves with various destructive acts of self-sabotage. Some, like Charles, are able to find a way to become more balanced—body, soul, and spirit. Others are not always so successful.

Johna

Let's look at a woman named Johna who, from all

appearances, was highly successful. She seemed very confident and fulfilled. She had an adoring husband and two wonderful children, and the family of four lived in a large house in the best part of their city. But Johna wasn't happy. Several challenges arose, however, that forced her to face a number of buried emotions.

"My dad was killed in a car wreck in Georgia," Johna was finally able to share with others. "I have lived with the fact that I actually prayed that he would die, for when I was a young girl, he abused me sexually. When we got the news of his tragic death, I was only eleven, but at that moment, I fully accepted the fact that it was all my fault. Worse, from that moment, I did everything in my power to wipe him, what he did to me, and his death from my mind. I even thought I was successful in doing that, as I enjoyed success in other areas of my life. Truth is, I spent my life trying to overcome the 'fact' that I killed my father through my childhood prayers. Only now, nearly forty years later, am I finally starting to come to grips with the fact that he was wrong, not me. I was reacting as any young girl would in such an abusive situation. The sad part is that I feel so cheated out of what should have been the best years of my life. No matter what I do or learn about myself, I still can't go back and undo the damage done to me and my family. The only thing I can do is go on from this point."

Abe

Abe's story has some similarities. He always dressed sharp, had a movie-star smile, and could charm the bark off trees. Sadly, he could never hold a job very long. He worked hard, obviously meant well, and always seemed to want to "turn over a new leaf." The problem always seemed to crop up, no matter where he worked, within a few months. He was simply his own worst enemy. The old phrase, "shooting himself in the foot," definitely applied to Abe. Anytime things started going well, he would suddenly get sick, or he would start performing poorly on his job by not paying attention or getting easily sidetracked. It almost seemed as if he intentionally talked himself out of doing well. The worst thing was that he never seemed willing to talk with anyone or do anything to get to the core of his problem. Frankly, in his mind, he didn't have a problem. It was always the fault of someone in management, or a coworker that he didn't get along with, or a laundry list of other reasons that kept sabotaging any long-term success. Worse, each time the inevitable job termination happened, he felt more and more like a failure and a victim. I wish I could offer a better report, but Abe continues his downward spiral and still refuses to seek any kind of help that could stop the desperate treadmill of defeat and destruction that continues ruining his life.

Background Influences

All of us—Charles, Johna, Abe, you, and me— must deal with the past before we can become successful in terms of body, mind, and spirit, especially as we seek to achieve true health, wealth, and wisdom.

Oliver Wendell Holmes, Jr., the late Supreme Court Justice and son of the famous physician, once said, "A page of history is worth a volume of logic."

You see, immediately after we are born, we are scrubbed clean, carefully checked over, and wrapped in a nice soft blanket. But soon after, it seems we are fitted for straitjackets. Of course, I'm not talking about real straitjackets— those designed to restrain people who have lost touch with reality and are restrained for their own safety and the safety of others. These straitjackets strap their arms to their torsos. I'm talking about another kind of straitjacket, not one you can see or touch, but a type that is powerfully restraining all the same.

These "straitjackets" are usually found on responsible people. But instead of preventing them from harming themselves, they actually prevent them from breaking free. If worn long enough, these straitjackets can ruin people by limiting their effectiveness and stifling their personal growth.

These straitjackets are "mind sets," or a collection of beliefs that most often are imposed on us by key members of our environment. The mind sets I'm talking about run much deeper than formal laws. They consist of customs and traditions. Our homes, schools, churches and synagogues, workplaces, and society in general are filled with authority figures who tell us what to do and when to do it. Their directives often are based on tradition. Following tradition for tradition's sake generally offers a structure too confining for effective performance and body, soul, and spirit harmony.

Philosopher and former Stanford University professor Dr. Willis Harman wrote:

> *"Each of us, as we naturally stand, is fragmented. We make choices at unconscious as well as conscious levels, and they are not necessarily in alignment. Viewed in this light, the psycho dynamic defense mechanisms can be thought of as unconscious choices. Repression is a choice to hide information from oneself; denial and resistance are choices not to perceive that which would imply change."*[7]

What do the pages of your history book reveal? What

have you repressed? What is fragmented? What "straitjackets" are you wearing?

Influences

Dr. Maxwell Maltz was a successful plastic surgeon who recognized the significance of the image we have hidden deep inside, which he detailed in his book Psycho cybernetics. Through experiences with his patients, he discovered that all people have a "mental blueprint or picture" of themselves, and they choose their actions and behaviors based on that image. In many cases, when Maltz performed surgery to remove scars or correct deformities, he noted that the patient's self-image improved dramatically within a relatively short period of time. As a result, so did their actions and behaviors. That led Maltz to conclude that individuals can improve their lives by improving the inner picture.

His research also revealed how people form those internal images. Certainly, it's rarely done consciously. Here are a few:

- Experiences even before birth. Ongoing research shows that unborn babies respond to outside communication. In Luke 1:39-45, Mary, the mother of Jesus, visited Elizabeth, and the baby Jesus leapt in her womb. Conversely, anger and sharp words can affect a baby adversely.
- Teasing by others when you are a child. Nicknames can be the worst, can't they? Especially, since you are so emotionally unprepared to deal with teasing. Usually, it seems, nicknames and teasing generally result from a person's negative features. Children who grow up being called "Fatty," "Four-Eyes," "Pig face," "Dummy," and "Spastic" often become self-conscious, defensive people. I was skinny as the proverbial rail, so

kids called me "Spider-legs Gene," and to this day, I tend to be self-conscious about my body.
- Parental or authority-figure rejection. An older person's opinion can carry a lot of weight with a young person, regardless of whether the opinion is true. Parents, siblings, coaches, and teachers can play an important part in building or destroying a person's inner view.
- Skills and abilities. People tend to focus on what they can't do rather than what they can accomplish. They tend to compare themselves with people who have developed the skills they lack. What makes it worse is that when you are a child, everything seems magnified. Your brother is the fastest runner in the neighborhood, and you aren't. Your sister makes the best grades in her class, and you don't. In my case, my Dad could fix anything with his hands—he had an exceptional mind for mechanical things, yet I seemed to be all thumbs, rather than a chip off the old block. As a result, all of us seem to find a way to feel that we don't "measure up," and we devalue ourselves. Of course, no one can measure up to the strengths of all the individuals he knows. To even think otherwise invites conflict. Unless we develop the tools to deal with these challenges, the things we perceive as shortcomings hold us back.
- Cultural differences. Many underprivileged people feel they're not as good as those who have many benefits. People of one race believe another has an unfair advantage. Ironically, many overprivileged children feel that they're not as good as their poorer peers who grew up on the streets and had to "pull themselves up by their own bootstraps." Black, white, brown, yellow, red, broke, rich, educated, underprivileged, tall, short,

fat, skinny—it almost seems as if we sometimes look for reasons to kick ourselves.

- Society's message. All societies have their codes. America functions on a work ethic. The harder you work, the more valuable you are. As a result, people who "march to the beat of a different drummer" might feel inferior if their lives don't revolve around their jobs. Or perhaps you have been looked down on because of your faith or rejected by people in a certain religion.
- Media. This is a powerful influence. It seems that the media's message is "Be slender, sexy, and beautiful." If you drink the right beverage or own the perfect car, you will be attractive and popular. If you are a star, life is a non-stop transition from fun times to fun times. Kids often believe this stuff. So do too many older people. Trust me, as one who has spent most of my life in television, it's an illusion. The people are often real, but the sets are fake, the limousines rented, and the words carefully scripted. Unfortunately, you don't know this as a young person when so much of your inner picture is being developed.
- Handicaps. People with physical and emotional challenges of any kind, especially those that people can see, often feel "unworthy" of success. That's a shame, because it's been proven that those who are challenged often outperform those who are not.
- Grading systems. While guidelines may be necessary to gauge a student's performance, such systems do not relate to a person's potential, nor do they encourage growth. Although a student who "fails" might be extremely capable in a nonacademic field, he or she might always carry the scars of a self-image that was wounded in the classroom. Grading systems exist also in business and industry. Individuals are graded on

how well they perform.
- Day-to-day experiences. It's the little things in life that people tend to remember—both positive and negative. Scorn, ridicule, and rejection can make strong impressions—as can positive events. Consider Steve Morris, a blind kid who sat in the back of the class with the rest of the so-called handicapped students during the 1950s. No one gave him much thought until the day the class hamster escaped from its cage. Teacher and students were beside themselves until blind Steve came to the rescue. With his acute sense of hearing, he quickly located the lost pet and became a hero. Steve never forgot that day, which proved to be a pivotal point in the forming of his self-image. And, by the way, "Stevie" changed his surname from Morris to Wonder, and began making recording history at the age of twelve, with such memorable hits as "Fingertips (Part 2)," "For Once in My Life," "Superstition," and "You Are the Sunshine of My Life."

Naturally, in all these areas, we tend to move toward the negative. Weeds are easier to grow than roses, for some reason. It's much harder to develop good inner images than negative ones. Often, regardless of age, we can be our own worst enemies.

Basic Truths

We have all been shaped by the attitudes, expectations, and values of people around us. And no matter how much we would like to think that we have the power to wipe our slates clean, from time to time, all of us are influenced by the past.

Worse, as historian George Santayana once wrote, "Those who disregard the past are bound to repeat it."

Before you can move into a life of health, wealth, and wisdom, you must realize several undeniable truths:

- You never start even with others. Some people are born with "silver spoons," others are deserted by their parents at birth. You have no control over this.
- Life, basically, makes no promise of being fair. You must accept this bittersweet fact before you can make positive steps toward success.
- You are influenced uniquely by past events. Two people can be born into the same city, have the same opportunities, and share many of the same experiences. Yet one of them may excel, while the other goes nowhere.
- You are largely a product of your environment. You can move to a new city where no one knows you, take a new job, form all new relationships, start an entirely fresh set of hobbies, and even have plastic surgery done on your face, but you can never completely start over. The reason is that each environment you are in puts its stamp on your body, emotions, and spirit. The more intense your feelings toward what happened in that environment, the more indelible that stamp tends to be.
- The past cannot be changed or controlled. You may alter your perception of past events, but you cannot change what has already happened.

If you grew up in an environment that placed a high value on financial success or academic achievement, you might feel like a failure even if you become a success in another field. Likewise, if you came from an underachieving background and family, you may feel tremendous feelings of guilt even if you become very rich. If you are a person who grew up in poverty, you may find it difficult to shake off the shackles of your past and become the real winner you are capable of becoming.

If you grow up poor, you may remember only the bad parts and work yourself to death, constantly worrying about not having enough money, no matter how much of it you amass. Or you might be the next Benjamin Franklin or Colonel Harlan Sanders.

Though past experiences are highly influential, you do not have to remain hobbled by them. If you are to succeed, you can acknowledge the events and people who have helped to shape your life, but you cannot use the past as a crutch or barrier any longer.

A FINAL NOTE

I am told that there is a unique way to trap monkeys—through very similar methods—whether on the islands of the South Seas or in India.

In India, for example, there are men who earn some extra rupees by trapping and taming monkeys to be sold as pets. Over the years, through trial and error, several ways have been devised to capture these primates, but the simplest method is said to be the monkey pot (similar to the hollowed out coconut in the South Islands). In a clearing, the trapper fastens a short piece of cord or thin chain to a stake or tree stump. To the other end, he attaches a small pot, one with a rather narrow neck. Into this pot he drops several nuts, and scatters a few more on the ground nearby. He then goes a short distance away to wait out of sight.

Soon a band of monkeys arrives and descends to feed. Before long, one of them discovers the contents of the pot. He puts his hand in easily enough, but having grasped the enticing snack, he cannot pull his clenched fist out through the narrow opening no matter how hard he struggles. In fear and panic, the trapped monkey creates quite a ruckus, which brings the trapper running with net and cage. The monkey's fate, for all his cleverness, is sealed.

At first glance it would appear that the villager is the trapper, the baited pot his trap, and the poor monkey his victim. No doubt the villager sees things the same way, and the hapless simian, were he able to speak, would likely agree. A closer look, however, shows a different perspective. The villager is not the trapper, nor the pot a trap, because there is nothing holding the monkey. He could very easily remove his hand from the pot and rejoin his kin in the freedom of the treetops if only he would unclench his fist and let go of the prize.

If he would only let go!

The monkey is being held prisoner solely by his mind. He has found some nuts. Though the jungle abounds with fruits and nuts and all kinds of foods, his conditioned reaction dictates that he must have these in the monkey pot as well. His narrow mind set is the only thing that imprisons him and prevents him from letting go—keeping him from seeing the absurdity of his predicament as well as the obvious way out of it.

What about you? What has conditioned you to act a certain way, even in a self-sabotaging manner? What do you have clenched in your fist that you refuse to release, even though letting go could signal the beginning of an entirely new level of freedom?

This business of letting go is so easy, and yet so hard, for monkey and for human being alike. We are both caught up in the same predicament. The details may be different, played out on higher levels of sophistication or complexity, but the end result is the same: enslavement by concepts and conditioning.

While the monkey is done in by its greed for a few mouthfuls of delicious nuts, we humans are done in by our greed for wealth, fame, power, status, pleasure, and shiny trinkets and toys, which we believe we absolutely must have and cannot live without. Even more fundamental, we become enslaved not so much by the material objects themselves, but by our attitudes and feelings toward them.

The ironic part of all this is that while we are frantically making more money, getting a bigger house, and another pricey car, hoarding more and better playthings, and trying to impress the neighbors, we have less and less time to enjoy the very things we are slaving for. The prize is not always what we expect, is it?

There is nothing wrong with wealth, but it must be balanced with health and wisdom. The same thing goes for the harmony of body, emotions, and spirit. Thankfully, balance and harmony are possible. You don't need to let anything hold you back from your God-given destiny. The plan? It begins just ahead.

Personal Health, Wealth, and Wisdom Insight

1. What are the critical hindrances to reaching your top three current goals?

2. How would your life change if you did reach all three current goals?

3. What three values or beliefs do you hold most dearly, and which of those three would you die for?

4. The most important idea I gained from reading Chapter Two is:

5. My plan for using this idea is:

Chapter Two Highlights

- You, no matter where you are or what you are doing with your life, are an amazing creation. You are the product of an incredibly complex design. Even a cursory glance tells you that any human—composed of mind, body, and spirit—form a magnificent organism capable of achieving almost unbelievable feats.

- So many people have become extraordinary wearers of disguises, even as they riddle themselves with various destructive acts of self-sabotage.

- All of us must deal with the past before we can become successful, in terms of body, mind, and spirit, especially as we seek to achieve true health, wealth, and wisdom.

- We have all been shaped by the attitudes, expectations, and values of people around us. And no matter how much we would like to think that we have the power to wipe our slates clean, from time to time, all of us are influenced by the past.

None of us can heal the things that life has done to us. They're done before we can realize what's being done, and they then make you do things all of your life until these things are constantly coming between you and what you'd like to be. And in that way you seem to lose yourself altogether.

Eugene O'Neill
Nobel and Pulitzer Prize-winning playwright

Chapter Three
Your Total Wellness Plan

The great thing in this world is not so much where we are, but in what direction we are moving.

Oliver Wendell Holmes

Let's focus on health as it relates to your total life plan. After all, everyone wants to be healthy, right?

Wrong?

Or maybe health is something akin to the old adage, "Everybody wants to go to heaven, but no one wants to die to get there." Perhaps everyone wants to be healthy, but they don't want to do what it takes to be well—body, emotions, and spirit. To do so requires a preventative, proactive lifestyle.

I'm reminded of a poem titled "A Fence or an Ambulance," written by Joseph Mains, which depicts the way too many people think. The verses of the poem describe a cliff where people would go to enjoy the view over a picturesque valley. However, the cliff held hidden dangers, for a duke and many of the town's peasants had slipped and fallen over the edge of the cliff to the valley below.

Some suggested that a fence be placed at the edge

of the cliff to protect unsuspecting individuals from the dangers below. Others said, "What we really need is an ambulance in the valley to care for the people who fall over the cliff."

After some discussion, it was determined that while the fence would be useful, the numbers of those who had already been injured pointed toward the need of an ambulance in the valley. After all, the cliff wasn't dangerous for those who were careful, but if anyone slipped over the dangerous cliff, it wasn't the slipping that hurt; it was the sudden stopping in the valley below! Therefore, an ambulance down in the valley was a must! So a decision was made, funds were gathered, and an ambulance was purchased.

Day after day, as the mishaps occurred and people fell from the dangerous cliff above, the rescuers would pick up the injured with the ambulance down in the valley and transport them to a place of safety where their injuries could be treated.

Eventually, a wise old man remarked, "It's a marvel to me that people will give more attention to repairing the injuries rather than dealing with the cause. They could put a stop to this problem by installing a fence near the edge of the dangerous cliff, for if people stop falling over the cliff, they wouldn't need an ambulance down in the valley!"

Public opinion rose up in response to the old man's remarks. "He's a fanatic! Do away with the ambulance? Never! People are being rescued as quickly as they fall. Why stop what we are doing and waste time building a fence? The ambulance in the valley is working just fine."

Benjamin Franklin would have concurred with the wise old man who wanted to build the fence when he uttered his famous quote: "An ounce of prevention is worth a pound of cure." How about you? Would you have voted for the fence or an ambulance? I am of the opinion that the fence is the better choice. Hopefully, you are too.

How often do we ignore the obvious? For centuries our ancestors sought mystical solutions to age and disease. During medieval times, people searched for the "philosopher's stone." New World Explorers sought to discover the magical "fountain of youth." Scientists have sought to tap into this mysterious dimension through wonder drugs and advanced surgical techniques.

We are no different. We want the magic pill that cures everything and makes us feel great, to boot! We want our youth back! We want to be healthy, no matter what we do to ourselves! Most of all, we want results right now! We have a "microwave mentality", and if we can get it from a bottle of pills or a machine, so much the better.

How ironic!

RESPONSIBILITY

What is health?

The words "health" and "healing" come from the Anglo-Saxon root, *hal*, which means "whole." "Holy" also is derived from that root. Sound health and wholeness—the balanced, harmonious functioning of body, mind, and spirit—is hardly a new idea, yet it is an unexplored frontier for a growing number of people who choose to live healthy and whole.

Clearly, from all the latest research on life and health, one fact stands like a glistening, inscribed monument:

You are responsible for your own choices. God has given you free will concerning your body, mind, and spirit.

Oh, how we hate taking responsibility for our choices. M. Scott Peck, M.D., the acclaimed psychiatrist and best-selling author of The Road Less Traveled, wrote:

> *"The difficulty we have in accepting responsibility for our behavior lies in the desire to avoid the pain of the consequences of that behavior... Whenever we seek to avoid the responsibility for our own behavior, we do so by attempting to give that responsibility to some other individual or organization or entity. But this means we then give away our power to that entity, be it "fate" or "society" or the government or the corporation or our boss. It is for this reason that Erich Fromm so aptly titled his study of Nazism and authoritarianism Escape from Freedom. In attempting to avoid the pain of responsibility, millions and even billions daily attempt to escape from freedom."*[8]

According to medical researcher Dr. Hilde Bruch, all patients come to therapists with "one common problem: the sense of helplessness, the fear and inner conviction of being unable to 'cope' and to change things."[9]

Quoting Peck:

> *"One of the roots of this 'sense of impotence' in the majority of patients is some desire to partially or totally escape the pain of freedom, and, therefore, some failure, partial or total, to accept responsibility for their problems and their lives. They feel impotent because they have, in fact, given their power away. Sooner or later, if they are to be healed, they must learn that the entirety of one's adult life is a series of personal choices, decisions. If they can accept this totally, then they become free people. To the extent that they do*

not accept this they will forever feel themselves victims."[10]

Victims? Helpless? There has to be a better way.

There is. Self-responsibility lies at the center of health and wellness. Notice this one glaring fact that is becoming more accepted by health practitioners all the time:

Your life and health depend upon factors largely under your own control.

Statistically, if you stop smoking, you can possibly add a decade or more to your life. Change your attitude, and you may be able to add another decade. Weight, alcoholic intake, exercise, sleep, and other factors primarily controlled by you are equally important. Our present behaviors accurately foretell future wellness.

For starters, here are several key points about healing and health:

1. Health is not always measured by the apparent absence of disease. Wellness has many standards that go beyond thermometer readings and diagnostic printouts.
2. Illness is not always a negative force. Like pain, it can be a beneficial network of signals, which are pointing to imbalance, unhealthy habits or changing patterns.
3. Healing is a multifaceted journey. Conventional medicine is not bad or good. Alternative health methods are not black or white. A true seeker of health—body, soul, and spirit—asks God for direction and guidance, and then utilizes the best of the best, regardless of the method's label or current popularity.
4. Health should not be left to chance or even to the so-called experts. If it is, you may be at the mercy of your genetics and gadgets. Worse, according to John

10:10, you cannot be passive about what happens to your body, emotions, and spirit, for Jesus Christ said: *"The thief does not come except to steal, and to kill, and to destroy. I have come that they may have life, and that they may have it more abundantly."*

Self-awareness and active participation in your own wellness influences all other facets of your health patterns. Self-awareness helps you realistically and accurately assess your situation. Participation forces you to focus attention on details or facts you may otherwise avoid.

POSITIVE STEPS

As we discussed in Chapter 2, the better you understand how the past continues to influence what you think and do in all areas of your life—certainly in terms of your health and wellness—the better equipped you will be to forge your own successful life. You can stop being a victim. You can make your own choices, with God's guidance.

Good choices are vital for good health. Your health is important for so many reasons. Of course, it prolongs life. No elaboration needed here. But subliminally, although not necessarily of lesser importance, is the fact that good health and a fit physique is a positive influence on a person's overall image of himself or herself. The better we look and feel, the better we deem ourselves. As a result, we perform better, and others respond to us more positively. It is a life-giving, positive cycle that anyone can achieve.

Here are nineteen basic steps to start you toward a life of great health:

1. *Take responsibility.*

    Take responsibility now for what you have been, what has happened to you, what you are right now, and what you will become. Don't spend your life blaming yourself or others. Simply take responsibility. Choose to live by your own values.

Of course, it is always easier to let others do your thinking for you, but you can be totally healthy, wealthy, and wise when you start taking responsibility for yourself and your own health.

2. *Set realistic goals for becoming healthy.*

One definition of health, the absence of sickness, is short and definitely understandable. Another, a bit more positive, is this: Wellness means that everything about a person—body, mind, and spirit—works in balanced harmony together.

Whatever your definition, set goals for yourself. All of God's creatures have ambitions.

People act the way they program themselves to act. The subconscious mind operates like a machine. It sends messages the individual has programmed it to send. If those messages are geared to success, the person will stand a good chance of succeeding. On the other hand, if those messages are related to failure, the person very possibly will fail.

People are destined to succeed at something. Whether we succeed at being a success or failure in our chosen endeavors depends on how ardently and frequently we pursue our ambitions and how well we use the time we can devote to them.

Would it be important to you to lose twenty pounds, gain more energy, and function effectively with only five hours of sleep? Would you like to be able to achieve more every day and still enjoy good health? This lifestyle can be yours if you're willing to set realistic goals for eating a balanced diet, exercising, and avoiding excesses.

Maintaining good health is critical to wellness in all areas of your life—body, soul, and spirit.

3. *Don't just break habits—replace them.*

Some of your ambitions might involve lifestyles that have no room for the habits you currently hold. For example, if you smoke three packs of cigarettes a day and have an ambition to compete in a triathlon, I'd say that you're going to have to give up something—either your cigarette habit or your ambition.

Bad habits can interfere with our ambitions. If upon arriving home, we habitually hit the couch and turn on the television, we can use a lot of time that might have been put to better use in a productive endeavor. Unfortunately, bad habits are difficult to drop. People become accustomed to acting out a practice, and old habits die hard. But they won't put up as much of a fight if you replace them instead. It all goes back to attitude.

Instead of dropping a habit, why not start a new one? Don't focus on the loss of an accustomed practice. Instead, focus on the gain of a new one. Cultivate tastes for water instead of soft drinks, fruits instead of sweets, fresh vegetables instead of cigarettes, exercise instead of inactivity. Habits can make or break us. And the power of bad habits is strong. But the power of good habits can help us succeed in our chosen endeavors. If you have habits that don't fit with your emerging image of what you want to become, find a good practice to replace the old ones.

4. *Eat right, and at the right times.*

Eating a balanced diet isn't enough for good

health. I have found that it's not only important what I eat, but when I eat it. For two years, I have followed a very interesting diet regimen that has helped me lose fifty pounds, while developing a much healthier lifestyle.

Starting in the mornings, I usually make a whey protein smoothie. This gives me a great deal of energy to make it throughout the morning. I usually try to eat something every two to three hours and the smoothie is a great start. A small snack mid-morning means I won't really go crazy at lunchtime either! For me, staying full and always incorporating protein every few hours makes the difference. As for lunch I really enjoy myself. Again sticking with a high protein meal balanced with carbohydrates is preferred. I always enjoy lean chicken or fish and while red meat is higher in fat, calories, and cholesterol I still enjoy the benefits of red meat as well. In the evening is when I really cut down the portion size and stick to lighter fare such as fish or salad. I have also discovered that eating earlier in the evening is much better for my body and I sleep better!

Reward yourself occasionally. I often do on weekends. Just knowing I can reward myself on the weekends helps me hold the course during the week. By choosing what foods to eat and when, I can function at my optimum level.

Also, I try not to eat anything after 9:00 pm. If I must have something, I'll have fruit or yogurt. The purpose for not eating late at night is so the body won't be digesting food and using energy while I sleep.

5. *Develop a total, lifelong program of both healthy eating and exercise.*

The two work together amazingly well. If you desire long-term wellness and fitness, then avoid extremes. Balance is the key.

Other than disease, there are only two basic ways to lose weight. One is to reduce food intake. Another is to increase caloric loss. I have learned from personal experience that the better way is to combine the two.

Much of the diet and exercise industry want to sell their systems, to the exclusion of common sense. You can buy crash diet plans, diet pills, complicated and expensive equipment, and so much more. There are plenty of people out there who prey on those who keep thinking that the next fad will be the one.

In my opinion the right way is through maintaining a proper diet and exercising sufficiently to burn up more calories than you take in. The wrong way is through "crash" or "fad" dieting, or depriving your body of a significant portion of its accustomed caloric intake.

Why? The body has the ability to accommodate changing conditions. When it's cold, we shiver to generate warmth; when it's hot, we perspire to release body heat and fluids. Likewise, when we starve ourselves, the body compensates by lowering its metabolism, which means that fewer calories will be burned. So the longer you diet, the fewer calories your body will burn. For the most part, any pounds lost will be limited to water weight and muscle, precisely the type of weight you don't want to lose.

And when you drop the diet and resume old eating habits, even more fat will be gained because the body is operating under a lower metabolic rate and burning fewer calories than before. Fad diets always include a decrease of caloric intake. And they deny certain essential foods or increase one or more foods.

By changing eating habits or maintaining a proper diet, the body will become accustomed to a lower level of caloric intake. Then regular exercise will keep the metabolic rate at a level high enough to burn calories, which means the body will lose fat. It's the perfect combination that works when you work it.

The challenge is obvious: Losing weight and keeping it off often happens over the course of time. But the longer it takes, the less painful the process will be. Cutting back just 100 calories per day can make a difference of more than 10 pounds within a year. Unfortunately, most people don't pace themselves. They start out "gung ho" and burn out when results don't rapidly materialize.

If you have more weight than you'd like, just remember that it didn't get there overnight, and it won't go away overnight. Exercise, revise your eating habits, and look at the venture as a long-term effort. Visualize yourself as being in shape, and allow your self-image to improve as the evidence of your hard work is revealed in your mirror by your new look. In time, your efforts will be rewarded.

6. *Exercise regularly.*

I just mentioned this, but it is worth repeating. The key word is regularly. The importance of regular exercise cannot be overemphasized.

Some of my friends and acquaintances prefer working out in the mornings. I prefer to work out in the evenings for several reasons. After putting in a full day, I'll go out for a walk or a light run. I personally believe that exercise is best in late afternoon or early evening, because the body's metabolism is winding down. At that point, exercise can "stoke the fire" to increase your body's metabolic rate, building energy and making it easier to be enthusiastic about continuing with the day. And I find that I can get some quality work completed in the evening hours. Also, exercise definitely helps me control my weight.

Others are just as convinced that morning or midday exercise is optimum, for a number of very good reasons. A good doctor friend of mine is often asked "What is the best exercise you can do for health and weight loss?" The answer is simple: The exercise that you'll do! The main thing is to exercise regularly, at least a half-hour, preferably an hour, three or more times each week.

7. *Take breaks.*

I try to work in an afternoon rest period of about 15 to 30 minutes. I have found that if I can get that much "quiet time" in the afternoon, it can add an hour or two onto my evenings. At a convenient time, somewhere between 3:30 and 5:30 p.m., if I can just lie down on a sofa, a bed, or even just rest my head on my desk with my eyes closed for 10 to 20 minutes, I will soon feel very refreshed and well rested.

Other people have to nap for an hour to feel rested. The main thing is to try to grab regular rest during the day, allowing yourself time to replenish your system.

8. *Be consistent with sleep.*

Experts say you should get at least 8-10 hours of sleep every night. I know people who seem to thrive on only 4-5 hours. Apparently people have different needs.

Whatever you need, here are a few suggestions for great, life-giving sleep:

- Stay in shape. Study after study makes it clear that regular exercise means better, more restful sleep. The body generally functions more efficiently in every area when it gets proper exercise. Oxygen flow to the bloodstream is increased, muscles are toned, and the amount of fat is reduced. Together, these benefits make sleep much more productive.

- Avoid eating before bedtime. People who make it a habit to have a "midnight snack" before retiring are not doing themselves any favors. As we've already seen, the body that must digest food while it sleeps is using energy that will likely be missed in the morning.

- Go to bed at the same time each night. This is where many people run into trouble. They will fall asleep at 9:00 p.m. while watching television one night; then go to bed at 1:00 a.m. the next. With no set bedtime, the body has no set schedule as a guide. A consistent bedtime is the key to setting a good sleep schedule. The body functions best when it gets the same amount of rest every day.

9. *Understand the law of small differences.*

Everyone wants to become instantly successful, but that simply isn't possible. When making changes in your life, be realistic. Don't expect too much too soon. The sheer burden of unrealistic expectations can frustrate you into inaction. It's better to set small, realistic and relatively easy-to-attain ambitions and increase them gradually, than to set a large ambition, only to become discouraged and lose motivation.

Small ambitions activate a positive self-image and our success mechanisms. For example, many dieters set unrealistic weight-loss goals. They go on crash diets for weeks, only to cave in eventually and revert to their old eating habits. But consider the person who approaches weight loss differently. By reducing caloric intake by 100 calories per day, he or she can lose 10 pounds in a year. Cut back by 200 calories per day, and 20 pounds can be shed within 12 months. One hundred to 200 calories is a relatively insignificant reduction in daily caloric intake.

Given time, insignificant contributions can amount to impressive results. In short, don't be afraid to think big, but also don't be afraid to think small. Big ambitions, including health, wealth, and wisdom, can be realized through small efforts.

10. Understand the importance of your attitude in everything.

A wonderful example is noted psychologist Viktor Frankl, a German Jew. He spent time during World War II in a concentration camp, where he made some interesting discoveries about human nature. He noted that the vile environment in which his peers were imprisoned tended to cause them to react in one of three ways to their plights. They could lash out at their captors and be killed on the spot, they could resign themselves to their cruel fates and wither away emotionally before expiring physically, or they could accept the reality of their circumstances and make the best of them by helping others cope with the dilemma. The people who chose the last option had a fighting chance at survival.

If Viktor Frankl and others could refuse to let such days prevent them from functioning positively and making healthy choices, why do we often let days marked by decidedly milder misfortunes blow our attitudes? Possibly because our attitudes are not in the proper shape in the first place.

What makes a day good or bad for you? Think about these contrasting perspectives for a moment:

Some people moan every Monday morning when, after enjoying a weekend break, they're faced with another five days "at the grind." Yet others appreciate Mondays for the opportunity to earn another week's income.

Some people view rain as a "downer," while others appreciate it because it nourishes the earth, contributes to healthy crops, and replenishes our water supply.

Some people view hot, sunny days as oppressive, while others view them as opportunities to get a suntan as they wash their cars, not at all minding if they get wet in the process.

Some people hate mowing their lawns, while others enjoy the opportunity for prolonged, mild exercise.

Short of the untimely and unexpected death of a loved one, virtually any situation can be viewed as good or bad. I've known people who were devastated upon breaking a relationship or losing a job, only to discover later that the incident served as the turning point of their lives. They were forced to make other plans that produced better, more rewarding situations.

11. Refuse to allow the drudgeries and boredom of life to drag you down.

If good and bad days are a matter of personal perception, then what about boredom and excitement? Doesn't the same principle apply?

Boredom is a choice. The best cure for boredom is to make use of your senses. Sight, hearing, taste, touch, and smell can reveal a new and exciting dimension to any situation perceived as boring. Use your God-given senses. Go outside and feel the sunshine. Open a window and listen to the rain as it hits the ground. Smell the freshness of the morning air, the fragrance of blooming pear blossoms, and the scent of freshly mown grass.

If it is a hot day, take a drive in the country. Give the air conditioner a break and open the car windows. Feel the breeze rushing inside as you drive on open roads. Enjoy the bouquet of honeysuckle and assorted wild flowers. Catch a whiff of tar and asphalt as you cross a bridge or railroad track, or sniff the crisp smell of gasoline as you pass a country service station. The world seems different when we use all of our senses. In fact, I believe that's a major reason why people suffer depression; they don't get enough sun and make full use of their senses.

We tune out many fine moments. For example, we don't savor the taste of a good steak, a juicy orange, or a glass of chocolate milk. We don't stop and listen to the symphonies of singing birds, chirping crickets, and heavy traffic. We don't appreciate the budding leaves. The difference is the interpretation of the events, and what a difference it makes in terms of total, abundant life.

12. Create your own environment for excitement about life.

Since excitement is a matter of perception, it stands to reason that excitement can be created. It is not necessary to wait for it to happen. Of course, people plan vacations and long weekends for an exciting change of pace, but there are other ways of creating excitement. You can begin by changing your patterns.

People often become bored with routine, regardless of what it involves. Try something new for breakfast, especially if you're accustomed to skipping the meal. Do something exciting with the extra time you've created by spending less time in bed. Read a book, write a letter, take a walk, exercise, watch a good movie on your DVD player—the options are numerous.

What a difference this can make in your whole outlook on life. Oscar Wilde said, "Consistency is the last refuge of the unimaginative." A certain degree of routine is necessary for a stable life, but too much of it can become monotonous. Variety is the spice of life.

13. Be thankful and appreciative for what you have and where you are right now in life.

First Thessalonians 5:18 tells us how: *"In everything give thanks; for this is the will of God in Christ Jesus for you."*

I have found that many people have problems counting their blessings. It is not that they feel as if they don't have any blessings to count, but they simply don't take the time to be thankful. If you have heat or air conditioning available in your dwelling and carpet on your floor, you have more than many people in the world. Be thankful that you have running hot water, a clean towel, and clean clothes. Many people don't.

If you can sit down to breakfast, be thankful that you're not a member of an underdeveloped country where any food, not just breakfast, is a rarity. Don't get me wrong. I'm not saying that the average person doesn't have problems. I'm just saying that perhaps we tend to allow our problems to overpower the positives. Don't be so preoccupied with life's negative aspects that you forget to appreciate its good ones. Be grateful to God for what you do have. That appreciation will blossom into an attitude of gratitude and carry over to being thankful to those around you.

14. Focus on your strengths and accomplishments.

One good way to keep a positive, healthy attitude about life is by focusing on your personal positives—your strengths and accomplishments. In my travels, I meet so many people who do just the opposite. They focus on their weaknesses and failures, which erodes their self-confidence. Inadequacy and ineffectiveness becomes a mind set, and their attitude suffers.

As a result, they won't attempt endeavors that could prove to be growing experiences because they fear failure. They refuse to "create possibilities" or subject themselves to experiences that would cause them to stretch their abilities and take risks. In short, they get stuck in a rut, which is nothing more than a grave with different dimensions!

Make a list of your personal strengths and accomplishments. It is the best way to reverse this negative situation. By focusing on positive points, you can create a mind set for growth and success.

As human beings, we're still learning how far we can go. Physiologists thought it impossible for a person to run a mile in four minutes. They thought the heart would literally explode under such strain. But British athlete Roger Bannister proved them wrong in 1954 by breaking the "impossible" barrier of the four-minute mile. Within months, others had done it too. When they saw that it actually could be done, they stopped setting limitations on their abilities.

Negative attitudes about ourselves place limitations on our abilities. By focusing on our strengths and past accomplishments, we can break through these limitations, become more effective, and develop a healthier lifestyle.

15. Create an environment conducive to a good attitude—then see what it does to your health and overall outlook on life.

Decorate your house with stimulating colors. Listen to motivational experts on CDs. Watch health-oriented television programs. Associate with people who have good attitudes, and avoid those who don't.

Healthy attitudes are contagious. So are unhealthy ones. Small-minded people can frustrate you, while broad-minded people challenge you to grow. Be selective in what you watch on television. Clip cartoons and art that express your outlook on life. Display photographs and posters of your role models.

16. Practice good grooming and hygiene.

Now, this might seem out of place in a book targeted primarily for adults, right? Wrong! You would not believe how many adults practice unhealthy personal habits.

At the risk of sounding like your middle school health teacher, let me point out the fact that hygiene is a critical factor in maintaining good health and wellness, especially in these four areas:

- Skin

Baths or showers are absolutely vital. Aside from keeping you clean, regular bathing helps keep pores open, which makes for healthier and better-looking skin. Regular exercise also can help improve the condition of your skin, because the body will perspire and eliminate many impurities. Experts also suggest that both men and women follow a regimen of gentle facial cleansers and lotions to maintain a soft and youthful look.

- Hair

Clean, neatly styled hair is critical to your overall health. Survey after survey of people in the workplace shows conclusively that one of the important factors in the way people respond to and react to you is because of your hair, specifically, proper style and neatness.

- Nails

Unkempt fingernails can ruin an otherwise fine impression of health and appearance. Keep your nails tastefully trimmed and cleaned. Don't bite them, whatever you do. This is such a simple thing, but it must be done to help you look your most healthy best at all times. You will feel better about yourself too.

- Teeth

While there can be many intestinal reasons for bad

breath, most bad breath results from poor dental care. Regular brushing and flossing not only keeps your mouth and teeth clean and fresh, but it also helps avoid the build-up of plaque, which can lead to gum disease and, if left untreated, loss of teeth. Research increasingly acknowledges the absolute need of dental care to maintain good health. In fact, according to the American Heart Association, there is mounting evidence that brushing, flossing and regular dental checkups may be at the heart of good cardiovascular health. Experts have known about the periodontal-cardiovascular link for over a decade.[11]

Stein said he regularly counsels patients worried about their risk for heart attack or stroke to incorporate good periodontal care in their preventive strategies, just as they would include exercise, healthy diets, and appropriate medications.

17. *Focus on your own uniqueness.*

Earlier in this book, I referred to the verse in Psalm 139:14, *"I will praise You, for I am fearfully and wonderfully made; marvelous are Your works, and that my soul knows very well."* Frankly, if you don't believe that God designed, created, and destined you in the most unique way (some call it intelligent design, but that's only part of the story), now is as good a time as any to recognize the ultimate truth.

All of us are unique individuals. There is no one in the world exactly like you. Yet many people develop poor attitudes and bad lifestyles for this very reason. They feel that they are different from the crowd.

In high school, this very feeling drives teenagers

crazy, because they think there is something wrong with them. Those who get free from this concept take on a much different frame of mind.

18. *Don't complain about things you can or cannot change.*

    Complaining about things that are within our power to change is the best way to develop a self-defeating attitude. Complaining about matters such as an undesirable job, a weight problem, or unhealthy habits subtly reinforces that we have no control over our lives, which is wrong.

    Truthfully, complaining is often a paltry attempt at venting frustration and, unfortunately, usually leaves you more frustrated than before. That doesn't help anyone, especially you.

19. *Be open to both traditional and alternative health care.* There is a world of healthy living available to you—everything from the latest medical and nutritional breakthroughs to such things as bodywork (deep tissue massage or reflexology, for example), chiropractic, vitamins, herbs, acupuncture, and so much more. And as the Chinese proverb says, "When the student is ready, the teacher will appear." There are prepared people who are ready to help you in your journey toward wellness. Finding them can be challenging, but rewarding as well.

    Mainly, be aware that both traditional and alternative health professions have both good and bad practitioners. Here are several guidelines that should be helpful, no matter what type of health care you are seeking:

- Beware of outrageous claims. The honest practitioner will usually understate potential benefits rather than raise unrealistic hopes.
- Beware of practitioners who rely on a single technique. They should always be open to more than one methodology or willing to refer you to someone else.
- Ask for references. The honest practitioner should respect your need to reach an informed decision.
- Don't accept complexity. You deserve a full explanation of what's happening. The "doctor knows best" attitude should not become "your herbalist knows best" or "How dare you question me, your massage therapist?" Total responsibility, remember?
- Look for the practitioner who considers you as a total person, not a collection of symptoms. He or she should listen attentively to you, respecting your concerns, ideas, and feelings.
- Don't pay outrageous fees. Even in alternative healing sciences, greed sometimes overshadows humane care. You get what you pay for, of course, but expensive does not always mean better. Better is better!
- Beware of the fanatic. The practitioner who refuses to consider any other types of treatment, either traditional or alternative, offers neither truth nor medicine nor wellness.
- Beware of combined effects. Individuals taking medication should be careful when they begin other forms of therapy. Whether you are a diabetic who takes insulin and goes to a massage therapist, a heart patient who is using nitroglycerine and also seeking help from an acupuncturist, or a pregnant herbalist going for prenatal care, talk with the practitioner about the possibility of combined effects.
- Accept responsibility. I cannot emphasize this enough.

Those in the healing sciences can help cure specific ailments, but they cannot give you health. Only God and your personal choices can do that.
- Educate yourself. Wellness—body, soul, and spirit—is a way of life, a vigorous search for well-being. It requires a commitment that goes beyond the timid norms of our drug-dependent society.

Who can help you toward wellness? In short, look for assistance from a health practitioner who works with you, not on you. A person who desires freedom needs no dictator.

Take responsibility now for what you have been, what has happened to you, what you are right now, and what you will become. Don't spend your life blaming yourself or others. Simply take responsibility. Choose to live by your own values.

Of course, it is always easier to let others do your thinking for you, but you can be totally healthy, wealthy, and wise when you start taking responsibility for yourself and your own health.

We all have control over our lives, yet some choose not to exercise it (literally!). Devote your energies to correcting undesirable situations you can change. Maintaining good health is critical to presenting your best appearance, not just to others but also to yourself.

God has made you distinctive, with your own unique blueprint. Your wellness is a series of choices that you make as you discover your uniqueness, not something that happens at random. To experience health, wealth, and wisdom, you must realize that this discovery is a life-long journey.

A FINAL NOTE

You are responsible for choosing good health or ill health. You can't use lack of information (information is readily available, much of it is already between the crown of your head and the soles of your feet) or an unwillingness to choose (you make vital choices every moment of your life) as excuses. Those excuses won't hold up any longer.

It's largely up to you. Robert Frost once said, "Something we were withholding made us weak until we found it was ourselves." Professionals in the healing sciences can help you recognize negative patterns and develop positive steps, but only you can set yourself free!

Simply stated, you are responsible for you. It is up to you to make changes in your lifestyle and environment that will contribute to better health. Practitioners and authorities are available in greater numbers today than ever, and you should use them whenever possible. Their primary goal, however, should be to teach you to understand your own body, emotions, and spirit.

No matter where you are in your journey, your work is just beginning. You see, deciding to find a better pattern for finding health, wealth, and wisdom is just the start. Finding a way to apply new truths to your life, throughout your life, is the challenge.

Did you know:
- The average diamond mining operation takes about 21 tons of rocks to produce one ounce of raw diamonds?
- Composed solely of carbon, a "diamond in the rough" is hidden in sedimentary rock (kimberlite) in proportions of one part diamond to 40 millions parts rock?
- With raw diamonds, no matter how great the poten-

tial, the real work—cutting and polishing—is yet to be done when the rock is unearthed?
- Once mined, the color, size, cutting, and even polishing are critical in the transformation of a diamond into a beautiful piece of jewelry. It is a delicate and tedious task and, depending on how well it is performed, the diamond will receive the appropriate grading, which determines its value.

Likewise, much in life depends on shoveling and overcoming obstacles before we can achieve shining success. Virtually every process in life—from mining diamonds to achieving health, wealth, and wisdom—includes first the spadework (insight into yourself, unearthing truth); then the real job of making something incredible out of the rough materials. Success, like life, is a process.

We often have a hard time accepting the fact that in order to be a success, many rocks have to be moved out of the way. As a consequence, our doubts and self-defeating habits emerge. Many of us finally get so frustrated with the rock removal that we never get any deeper insights than the mere surface. Others of us get so preoccupied with removing rocks that we tend to forget our real job of developing into all that God has created us to be.

Personal Health, Wealth, and Wisdom Insight

1. How healthy are you—body, emotions, and spirit?

2. What area of the three requires the greatest amount of work?

3. What is the most destructive health habit you have?

4. What positive habit could you develop to replace the negative one?

5. What are some specific targets you would like to set for yourself, in terms of health and exercise?

6. What would your life be like in one year if you could be successful in reaching your targets?

Chapter Three Highlights

- Your life and health depend upon factors largely under your own control.

- Good choices are vital for good health.

- Develop a total, lifelong program of both healthy eating and exercise. The two work together amazingly well.

- Be open to both traditional and alternative health care, but also beware and be informed.

- No matter where you are in your journey toward health and wellness your work is just beginning.

One man gets nothing but discord out of a piano; another gets harmony. No one claims the piano is at fault. Life is about the same. The discord is there, and the harmony is there. Study to play it correctly, and it will give forth the beauty; play it falsely, and it will give forth the ugliness. Life is not at fault.

Author Unknown

Section 2

Wealth

Pronunciation: `'welth also 'weltth`
Function: *noun*
Etymology: Middle English *welthe*, from *wele* weal

1. *obsolete* : *weal, welfare*
2. : abundance of valuable material possessions or resources
3. : abundant supply : profusion
4. **a**: all property that has a money value or an exchangeable value **b** : all material objects that have economic utility; *especially* : the stock of useful goods having economic value in existence at any one time <national *wealth*>[12]

Chapter Four
True Riches

If your daily life seems poor, do not blame it; blame yourself that you are not poet enough to call forth its riches; for the Creator, there is no poverty.

Rainer Maria Rilke
Considered to be the German language's greatest twentieth-century poet

---

If your future could be the way you wanted it to be, what would it be like? As a simple exercise, supposing your future could be the way you'd like, think of all the things you dream about obtaining, achieving, or accomplishing in your lifetime and list those things on paper.

Let's try another pointed question: Imagine that you only have a week to live. What dreams would you eliminate from the list? Are there any desires you would add to it?

Whatever you wrote for either question, I'll bet it looks good to you. And why shouldn't it? The list is a recording of the way you'd like your future to be if it could be any way that you want.

So my question to you is, why can't it be? Why can't the future be the way you would like? There's no reason that your future can not be of your own making. In fact, that's exactly what it will be!

You hold the keys to your tomorrows. The future is not simply a set of events waiting to happen. It's not a script with your name on it that you're predestined to follow. The future can and will be whatever God has designed for you to become, as you work out His plan in your life.

What's the difference between people who fulfill their destinies and those who don't? The only significant difference is that people who become all they were designed to be are willing to set challenging and rewarding goals and work toward those goals. Understanding that fact alone is worth vast riches to you!

TRUE RICHES

There is a passage in the New Testament that defines true riches:

"And I say to you, make friends for yourselves by unrighteous mammon, that when you fail, they may receive you into an everlasting home. He who is faithful in what is least is faithful also in much; and he who is unjust in what is least is unjust also in much. Therefore if you have not been faithful in the unrighteous mammon, who will commit to your trust the true riches? And if you have not been faithful in what is another man's, who will give you what is your own? No servant can serve two masters; for either he will hate the one and love the other, or else he will be loyal to the one and despise the other. You cannot serve God and mammon."

Luke 16:9-13

The Lord Jesus indicates that there are "true riches," something more desirable than abundance of money. Obviously, from what the Master said, every person has to choose whether they will serve God or serve themselves by serving money. People do this by basing their decisions on how much they personally will get out of something. To determine how much you are serving money, ask yourself what weight money has in the decisions you make. When deciding whether to do something, is money the main thing you consider? Would you turn down a more lucrative job offer unless you believed God was leading you to accept that job? Or would you make an automatic, no-brainer decision simply because the job offered more money?

You see, the secret of true riches is the bare-bones fact that money is a poor god. Money can be a handy tool, but money is a poor master. Looked at from a long-term perspective, money is also a poor provider. Money cannot supply many important things. For example, money may buy companionship, but it cannot buy love. Money may buy a house, but it cannot buy a home. Money may buy a bed, but it cannot buy rest. Money may buy you thrills, but it cannot buy continuing satisfaction. Money may buy you food, but it cannot guarantee that you will have the health to eat it. Money may buy you doctors, but it cannot buy you health.

Money cannot buy you peace of mind and freedom from fear and worry, nor can it buy you protection from every possible calamity.

Face it—history's pages are filled with numerous accounts of times when the money people trusted in and built their lives around suddenly became worthless. The same thing can and will happen again. But here's the good news: Everything that money cannot do, God can do.

Only God is dependable: *Command those who are rich in this present age not to be haughty, nor to trust in uncertain riches but in the living God, who gives us richly all things to enjoy* (1 Timothy 6:17).

God loves you and desires the best for you. He certainly has nothing against true riches. After all, He is the Creator. God's Word gives us key promises that relate directly to His blessing. Never forget that we surrender in obedience not in order to be blessed, but in expectation of blessing because we know of the Father's great love and generosity for His children. He promises:

- Multiplication—Then God said, *"Let Us make man in Our image, according to Our likeness; let them have dominion over the fish of the sea, over the birds of the air, and over the cattle, over all the earth and over every creeping thing that creeps on the earth." So God created man in His own image; in the image of God He created him; male and female He created them"* (Genesis 1:26-27).
- Favor—*"And the Lord had given the people favor in the sight of the Egyptians, so that they granted them what they requested..."* (Exodus 12:36).
- God's face will shine on you—*"The Lord bless you and keep you; the Lord make His face shine upon you, and be gracious to you; the Lord lift up His countenance upon you, and give you peace. So they shall put My name on the children of Israel, and I will bless them"* (Numbers 6:24-27).
- Power to get wealth—*"And you shall remember the Lord your God, for it is He who gives you power to get wealth, that He may establish His covenant which He swore to your fathers, as it is this day"* (Deuteronomy 8:18).
- Good success—*"This Book of the Law shall not depart*

from your mouth, but you shall meditate in it day and night, that you may observe to do according to all that is written in it. For then you will make your way prosperous, and then you will have good success" (Joshua 1:8).
- Fulfilled promise—*"Blessed be the Lord, who has given rest to His people Israel, according to all that He promised. There has not failed one word of all His good promise, which He promised through His servant Moses"* (1 Kings 8:56).
- Prosperity—*"Let them shout for joy and be glad, who favor my righteous cause; and let them say continually, 'Let the Lord be magnified, Who has pleasure in the prosperity of His servant.' And my tongue shall speak of Your righteousness and of Your praise all the day long"* (Psalm 35:27-28).

True riches, indeed!

As we live the truth of the promises of the Word, the Father delights to hold out for us not only that we partake of the divine nature, but also that we can ...*escape the corruption in the world caused by evil desires* (2 Peter 1:4 NIV). Truly, *"...we are more than conquerors through Him who loved us"* (Romans 8:37).

Every good thing came from Him. However, the reason God does not want us to trust in riches is because they are uncertain and will fail us. Only God is certain. Therefore, we should trust in His Word, for that trust will not lead to disappointment: For the Scripture says, *"Whoever believes on Him will not be put to shame"* (Romans 10:11).

So how do we access these true riches in everyday terms? We do it by being diligent as we seek to fulfill our God-given destiny.

ENDLESS POSSIBILITIES

When you stopped for a few moments at the beginning of this chapter and wrote down your ambitions, you were actually opening up to the possibilities in your life. You were giving voice to your ambitions, which are the seeds of fulfillment and happiness. But whether these ambitions and possibilities ever become reality depends on whether or not you are able to establish and follow a plan of action.

To do that, you must know what is truly important in your life. Here are a few of the primary areas you should consider:

- *Body*

To chart your future, you must have one. There are three good ways to maximize chances that you'll have a future. One is to avoid dangerous situations, such as reckless driving. Two is to limit or eliminate certain vices that would jeopardize your health. And the third way to maintain good health is by engaging in moderate to vigorous exercise for 30 minutes to an hour, at least three times a week.

By taking care of yourself, you can maximize the remainder of time you have left to pursue and achieve your ambitions. Of course, this area also could include ambitions to complete a triathlon or to develop a body that could adorn the cover of a muscle magazine. But for most people, maintaining a good weight level and taking care of the body itself is sufficient.

- *Emotions*

Of course, there is more to life than fitness and money. Activities with our family and friends are important for our emotional development and satisfaction.

- *Spirit*

   We have discussed the fact that human beings are three-dimensional—body, emotions, and spirit. Certainly the last category is the most important of all and should never be overlooked by the person who wants to develop a full life. Strong spiritual development is the most needed source of power.

In addition, you should also consider:

- *Career*

   Your career obviously will mean a great deal to you. Careers give us purpose, help build our self-esteem, and provide us with income that we can apply toward necessities and desires. If you don't have any career ambitions, let me suggest that you might be in the wrong career, and I would heartily advise you to look into the possibility of establishing another.

- *Educational/intellectual*

   Although we discussed the fact that attitude plays a significant role in performance, that is certainly not an attempt to understate the importance of knowledge. Knowledge not only makes performance possible, but it gives us the self-confidence that contributes to a positive attitude. People who desire to improve upon what they do should have educational goals to coincide with their ambitions for personal advancement.

- *Financial*

   If you want to be among the 3 percent of people who are self-sufficient upon retirement, then you might consider making plans now regarding your finances. The same is true if you ever consider a major acquisition such as a home or your own business. Likewise, if you want to take an extended cruise to some exotic tropical island. Whatever you want out of life will cost you something, primarily money. Having lots of money is wonderful, as long as the money doesn't have you.

- *Relationships*

Relationships make life worth living. Everyone needs support systems—especially family and friends. Power and success have little or no meaning at all without people in your life with whom you can share the results of your achievements. Success without people to share it is painfully empty. No one is an island. We depend on effective interaction with others to build families, friendships, and business associates. The person who can't build relationships probably won't be able to build a fulfilling life.

- *Recreational*

Even common radio batteries need time for recharging, so they can continue to offer maximum performance. The same is true for people. All work and no play can be hazardous to a person's overall development and continued happiness.

- *Hobbies and other interests*

We play many roles in life, and some of our roles are neither at home nor in the workplace. We often find ourselves playing roles in churches and volunteer organizations, and many of us have hobbies we pursue in our spare time that add meaning to our lives. Achievements and distinctions we wish to gain through our avocations can be included in goal planning.

- *Behaviors*

We all have behaviors we wish to improve. This is

especially true of powerful people, who are mindful of the negating effect that inappropriate behaviors have on individual power. When habitual inappropriate behavior tends to threaten overall effectiveness, powerful people set goals to change.

- *Work habits*

The category of work habits deals with success or failure. For example, a person with a tendency to procrastinate might set a goal to overcome the habit by learning good time-management skills.

It is important to realize and clarify your ambitions in all areas of life. Before you can become successful, it is important to identify what success and fulfillment mean to you. After all, if you don't identify your idea of success, how can you hope to reach it?

GETTING THERE

Clarifying your concept of success, however, is only the first step. The real work lies in bringing the idea to reality. Depending on your ambition, bringing it to reality can be extremely difficult.

As noted television minister and motivational speaker Dr. Robert Schuller says, "Yard by yard, life is hard; inch by inch, it's a cinch!" No matter how grand your ambition, you can break it down into a series of objectives that can guide you to success.

Let's assume that your ambition is to start your own business, but at this point, you lack the experience and capital. Using ambition as an example, let me show you how it can be divided into a series of smaller objectives.

- *Long-range goals*

These goals define the ambition—to start a business

and make it successful. Of course, this might require a considerable amount of capital that you'd have to raise before starting the endeavor. Although time lengths for long-range ambitions can vary, they generally require three to five or more years to accomplish.

- *Medium-range goals*
These goals might include earning a college degree or getting necessary experience to qualify you as an effective business person in your chosen field. Also, a good intermediate goal might be to amass a certain amount of capital to show that you're on your way to accumulating enough money to start a business. Time lengths can vary for intermediate ambitions, but they generally run one to three years, perhaps more.

- *Short-term goals*
In this case, a short-term ambition might be enrolling in school, starting a job designed to give you experience, and making a significant contribution to a fund earmarked for your new business start. Short-term ambitions generally run from about a month or two to a year.

When you break down your goals into a sequence of smaller objectives, it will be easier to achieve your ultimate desires. Rather than being overwhelmed by an enormous long-range ambition, you'll be focusing on a series of individual steps designed to bring the long-term ambition to reality.

FOCUS

People who are able to focus on their objectives most often are successful, because they concentrate on activities that will lead to successful accomplishment. By making the current objective their mission, they tend to avoid activities that don't apply to their ambitions.

For example, writing a book might be a short- or medium-range goal. But when you get involved in the actual writing, you have to focus on the project in more ways than you previously realized. The book takes on a life of its own. Suddenly you are researching, making notes, arranging facts, and gathering illustrations. Then you begin to realize that there is little time for television, radio, and a host of other activities you may be accustomed to doing. As a result, you begin making progress, your self-confidence increases, and you become even more focused.

Let me offer some tips on how to focus on your goals for maximum results.

1. *Write down your goals, and read them daily.*

    Some people do this on their computer. Others do them on sticky notes. Maybe you prefer writing your goals on three-by-five index cards. With one goal per card or note, the goals are easier to handle and read.

    By reading them every day, you will remind yourself of their meaning in your life. Believe me, this step is important. Life is full of urgencies that can overshadow your ambitions if you are not careful. Daily reading keeps them uppermost in your mind.

2. *Weed out insignificant activities.*

    It always seems that you need more hours in the day to get things done, but the only way that happens is when you are able to make critical choices about eliminating activities that aren't pertinent to your goals. Get proficient at asking the question, "Is this activity helping me to reach my most valued goals?"

3. *Reserve time for your most important ambitions.*

    If an ambition is worth pursuing, it's worth devoting time to. Set aside time in your life, preferably when you won't be interrupted, for the pursuit of your most driving ambitions.

4. *Seek the company of people with similar goals and ambitions.*

    You can get a ton of support and million-dollar ideas from people whose ambitions are comparable to yours. Also, it's a good idea to read about people who have been successful in your chosen field. If possible, talk with them. You could learn something in a few minutes that otherwise might have taken months, if not years, to discover for yourself. In the end, birds of a feather really do flock together.

5. *Get great at imagining that you already have achieved the ambition.*

    Visualize yourself already there. By seeing yourself as successful, you will send powerful health, wealth, and wisdom messages to your brain. These messages will positively influence your inner-image, which will encourage you to operate at peak performance. As a result, your chances of succeeding will be greatly increased.

6. *Concentrate on short-term objectives.*

    People who concentrate on their long-term desires often become frustrated and give up. But people who concentrate on their short-term objectives usually become successful. By concentrating on the short-term goal, the long-range goal will take care of itself.

If you find this difficult, try to recognize satisfaction in completing short-term objectives. For example, people who exercise only to improve the shape of their bodies tend to become frustrated. After all, it takes bodies a long time to take on different shapes. But people who exercise because it makes them feel better right now will usually stick with it to reap the reward of a better-looking body.

7. *Keep your eye on the prize.*

The best way to maintain enthusiasm is by keeping in mind your desired reward. This also allows your built-in health, wealth, and wisdom mechanisms to go to work for you. When frustration and despair set in, renew your efforts by focusing on your ultimate ambition.

Post photographs of tangible items you aspire to own, such as cars, boats, homes, or charitable gifts. Place photographs around you of desired ends such as finishing that marathon, reaching the top of the mountain, going on that missionary trip, receiving that Grammy or Emmy, wearing the gold medal, or sitting behind the desk as a CEO. All of these can help inspire you to achieve far more than anything you previously dreamed possible.

8. *Inner-talk yourself into fulfilling your God-given destiny.*

You talk to yourself constantly, whether you realize it or not. Most of the time people are not aware that they are talking to themselves. It just comes automatically. You are talking to yourself nearly every moment of every day. Since the human mind tends to go toward the negative, most of what you say to yourself

is crippling:
"I can't..."
"If only I were..."
"What an idiot I am..."
"Why can't I be more like...?"
"I could never make that work..."

The language of the mind can be controlled to work for us, helping to make us into the people we want to be. King Solomon, whose name is synonymous with wisdom, wrote, *"Death and life are in the power of the tongue..."* (Proverbs 18:21). In Proverbs 15:4, he also said, *"The tongue that brings healing is a tree of life, but a deceitful tongue crushes the spirit"* (NIV).

Whatever you speak out of your mouth influences your thoughts. Seneca once said, *"Speech is the index of the mind."* Jesus put it this way, *"Out of the abundance of the heart the mouth speaks."* (Matthew 12:34). Whatever you begin focusing on is what you speak, and whatever you speak, your mind believes. The spoken word reinforces the image in your mind, and ultimately that mental picture will probably become reality. Have you ever heard someone say, "I just can't lose weight. I've tried every diet that ever came along, but I don't lose. I gain." And they do!

You see, people generally get what they desire, and those desires surface in the form of the way they talk. Somehow, a person's words unconsciously tap into his or her deepest desires.

Charles Capps, in his best-selling book, *The Tongue—A Creative Force*, shares this thought-provoking analogy:

> *"A few years ago I came upon the scene of an accident. A car had gone out of control and cut off a power pole. The high line wire was hanging*

about three feet above the ground. Many people had stopped and gotten out of their cars. They were standing no more than three feet away from that live wire, thinking that it was insulated, or that the power was cut off. But this was not true; the wire was "live" with over 17,000 volts of electricity. I watched from my car, a safe distance away, as the ambulance attendants carried a woman on a stretcher up the highway embankment. As they crawled under the power line one of them got too close, and the electrical current arced to his body like a lightening bolt. He died instantly and the other attendant was critically injured. He violated the natural law that governs electricity. No doubt he did it in ignorance, yet it was fatal. Lack of knowledge did not stop the electrical force. It continued to work. It was the same force that cooked his meals, heated his house, and washed his clothes. It was created to work for him to make life more enjoyable. The very reason for its existence was to supply his needs, but when he violated the law that controlled that force, it destroyed him."[13]

So it is with the way you talk to yourself. If you want to change, try these basic self-talk principles:

- Always phrase your inner statements with "I." You can think up self-talk statements for only one person—yourself.

- When you catch yourself making negative statements, stop and turn them into positive affirmations. Instead of saying, "I am afraid of..." or even, "I will not be afraid of....," say, "I really enjoy...."

- Keep your inner-talk in the present tense. Make it true for you now, not in the future or in the past. Especially be careful about saying, "I am going to . . ." since you will likely never get to that point. Instead, say "I am..." A present-tense form allows you to experience right now what it will be like once you actually realize your dreams.

- Make your inner statements enjoyable and exciting. Let your words fill all your needs and desires. Be positive!

- Write your inner-speech statements, perhaps using the notebook you have kept for each chapter's Health, Wealth, and Wisdom Insights. By writing these sentences, you crystallize your thoughts. By reading the notes you have written, you reinforce those thoughts, and those thoughts will influence your actions.

- Use a mirror, as often as possible, when you make your positive inner statements. Try to do this for at least a few minutes each morning, night, and sometime during the day. Become your own best friend and encourager!

Does it work? Dr. Shad Helmstetter, noted psychologist and founder of Self-Talk Systems, Inc., writes, "Your own self-talk to your own inner self is, and always will be, your surest form of inner defense and inner strength. Combine that with your personal source of spiritual strength—and no one, nothing, can override it."[14]

Here is my challenge to you: Use positive inner-talk for one month, every day, and your life will change forever!

Focus! As the Nike advertisement urges, "Just do it!" The more you focus on reaching your goals, the more you will be surprised at how amazing, responsive, and destined for greatness you really are. Focusing is critical to achieving your goals and ambitions. If something is important enough to excite you, then it is important enough to receive your best efforts.

A FINAL WORD

Remember, God desires the best for you. How can you desire anything less than what He has destined you to become?

Take a look at Malachi 3. There are seven blessings mentioned in Malachi 3:10-12 that extend to every area of your life—body, emotions, and spirit:

- God will open for you the windows of heaven.
- God will pour out for you such blessing that there will not be room enough to receive it.
- God will rebuke the devourer for your sakes.
- The devourer will not destroy the fruit of your ground.
- Nor shall the vine fail to bear fruit for you in the field.
- All nations will call you blessed.
- You will be a delightful land.

It is so important to recognize here that the Lord blesses us spiritually and materially. To ignore one or the other is to sell God short and not be honest with Scripture.

Seek God's will in your life. Recognize the God-given ambitions that He has placed inside you. Set up an action plan for reaching your goals. Then focus on becoming all you are designed to be. That is the trail to true riches. That is the path to health, wealth, and wisdom!

Personal Health, Wealth, and Wisdom Insight

In the beginning of this chapter, I asked you a couple of questions. Take a few moments to summarize your answers and add any additional thoughts:

1. If your future could be the way you want it to be, what would it be like? As a simple exercise, supposing your future could be the way you'd like, think of all the things you dream about obtaining, achieving, or accomplishing in your lifetime, and list these on paper.

2. Imagine that you only have a week to live. What dreams would you eliminate from the list? Are there any desires you would add to it?

Chapter Four Highlights

- God loves you and desires the best for you. He certainly has nothing against true riches. After all, He is the Creator. God's Word gives us key promises that relate directly to His blessing in your life.

- Before you can become successful, it is important to identify what success and fulfillment mean to you.

- Set long-, medium- and short-range goals for yourself. Then put together an action plan for reaching your goals and ambitions.

- The more you focus on reaching your goals, the more you will be surprised at how amazing, responsive, and destined for greatness you really are. Focusing is critical to achieving your goals and ambitions.

The riches that are in the heart cannot be stolen.

Russian Proverb

Chapter Five
Time - Our Most Valuable Asset

Dost thou love life? Then do not squander time, for that is the stuff life is made of.

Benjamin Franklin

The first law of science states that matter can neither be created nor destroyed. But what about time? Does the law apply to time? After all, time is not matter. It can neither be seen nor touched, and it doesn't take up space. So we can assume that the law doesn't apply to time. Of course, that's a faulty assumption. Time might not be matter, but it certainly cannot be created or destroyed. All people have 24 hours per day at their disposal—no more and no less.

But can time be wasted? You bet it can. Studies show that most employees use only a fraction of an eight-hour day efficiently. Some estimates say that white-collar workers waste an hour for every hour of productivity. If those estimates are true—and I don't doubt them—think of how America's productivity could rise if employees would put time to better use.

Consider how much your time is worth.

Time Value Chart

ANNUAL INCOME	EACH HOUR IS WORTH	EACH MINUTE IS WORTH	AN HOUR A DAY FOR A YEAR
$10,000	$5.16	$.0864	$1,259
$12,000	$6.16	$.1024	$1,503
$14,000	$7.16	$.1192	$1.748
$16,000	$8.16	$.1360	$1,992
$20,000	$10.32	$.1728	$2,518
$25,000	$12.81	$.2134	$3,125
$30,000	$15.37	$.2561	$3,750
$35,000	$17.93	$.2988	$4,375
$40,000	$20.64	$.3596	$5,036
$50,000	$25.62	$.4268	$6,250
$100,000	$51.24	$.8536	$12,500
$200,000	$102.48	$1.7072	$25,000

Note: The table is based on 244 working days of 8 hours each.

Time, regardless of where you are on the ladder of success, is valuable, yet time passes at the same rate for everyone, regardless of who they are or where they live. Time might not be matter, but it matters a great deal when it comes to realizing our ambitions, because a major difference between successful people and people who fail is the way they use time.

Management expert and best-selling author Peter Drucker once said, "Time is the scarcest resource. Unless it is managed nothing else can be managed." Actually, despite these helpful words, you cannot manage time at all, for you have no control over it. All you can do is manage your use of time. Therefore, time-management is actually self-management.

MANAGING TIME

What would you do with one more hour per day? Let's consider the possibilities. You could apply the additional sixty minutes to work, leisure, exercise, or your own pursuits. If you'd like, you could spend the extra hour in bed.

But we've already determined that time can't be created, so we can't really add an hour to our days. Time management, however, is possible through self-management. By wisely investing your time, you can effectively increase the amount of value to each day.

That's what self-management is all about. True, your day is only going to last 24 hours, no matter how much or how little you do. But by making the most efficient use of your time, you'll be able to schedule more activities into your days. As a result, you'll be more productive and effective—two qualities that always are in demand with businesses. But, more importantly, by using time efficiently, you can sooner achieve your objectives. And when your objectives hinge on deadlines, efficient use of time often makes the difference between whether or not you achieve them at all.

TIME-WASTERS

First, you should identify and eliminate wasteful habits that rob you of your most vital possession—your very own life—and give little or nothing in return. Consider these research findings:

- The average worker wastes 40 percent of a typical day.
- The average manager is interrupted every 3 to 5 minutes, and it takes up to 20 minutes after the interrup-

tion to get back on track.
- At best, only two out of every 10 people can be considered good time managers.

If you want to gain control of your time (and your life), you simply must identify and eliminate the time-wasters that steal your most prized possession, the invaluable moments of your life. To get started, study this list of the most common ways people waste time:
- Unnecessary paperwork and mail shuffling
- Internet abuse
- Telephone misuse
- Excessive socializing
- Procrastination
- Careless mistakes
- Ineffective communications
- Trying to complete tasks for which you don't have enough information
- Daydreaming
- Extra-long breaks
- Refusing to say no to things that interfere with your priorities
- Doing unnecessary routine work—just because you have always done it
- Unnecessary distractions or interruptions
- Unnecessary meetings, or meetings that last too long
- Failure to delegate tasks to capable people
- Lack of self-discipline in matters of time
- Failure to set priorities
- Lack of job knowledge Failure to use time-management aids (voicemail, e-mail, message centers) to full advantage
- Poorly designed, time-wasting systems or procedures
- Failure to insist that coworkers carry their part of the

load

Once you have identified your own time-wasters, eliminate them. You have everything to gain.

PLANNING—THE KEY TO TIME MANAGEMENT

There is nothing that will enhance your self-management efforts more than planning. In their haste to save time, many people leap into a project without planning. But they generally find that a lack of planning leads to inefficient use of time.

Planning is the way to make sure that all necessary items are secured before the actual execution phase begins. As a result, a great deal of time can be saved. Increasing planning time reduces execution time of a project and, as a result, decreases total time for the project. Consider the delays that might result when, in the midst of a project, you discover that vital information is missing, or that essential material is not on hand. It's generally accepted that one hour of planning saves four hours of execution.

Also, consider what happens when a two-hour task is attempted during a one-hour time frame. Either the task must be shelved until it can be completed, or whatever is scheduled for the next hour must be postponed. Without proper planning, people generally find themselves pinched for time, which means the project might be completed hurriedly—and ineffectively.

Also, planning is the step during which your activity list is compiled. Without serious planning, you'll spend your days responding to events as they materialize, rather than scheduling them to your best advantage.

So plan your days ahead of time, either first thing in the morning or during the prior evening. If you're not accustomed to planning, start small and increase as you become more comfortable with it. Plan half a day, and then work up to a whole day. Then you can tackle a week...then a month. What ambitions will you attack? What projects will you begin or end? Who will you contact? When you determine events that are urgent and plan them accordingly, you can become better aware of how much discretionary time you'll have at your disposal.

So remember the five essentials for planning—*knowledge or information, skills or know-how, attitude or willingness to perform, materials and tools, and time.* But perhaps most important of all is to act. All of the others do not amount to much unless we put action into our ambitions. Consider each of these when planning to ensure smooth execution.

TIME MANAGEMENT TIPS

If you want to perform successfully in all of your roles in life as you seek balance between body, emotions, and spirit, it will be to your benefit to practice sound self-management principles. If you already do this, then you're on your way to realizing your ambitions. If you don't, you might find getting started the toughest hill to climb. Let me share fifteen simple ways to begin practicing proper self-management:

- *Develop an acute awareness of time.*

Most of us have little concept of how much time it takes to do any given task. We almost always underestimate. Thus, we tend to not allocate enough time for almost every task we do, and then to feel frustrated because we can't get it all done.

- *Keep a time log.*

One of the best ways to develop an acute awareness of time is through a time log. You see, money and time have a way of disappearing, and the person who runs out of them often can't account for where those assets went. Until you know exactly where your time is going, it will be difficult to put it to better use. That is why a time log is important. Record how you spend each quarter-hour. Discipline yourself to make an entry in your log every 15 minutes. Don't wait until the end of the day to reconstruct your actions. First, the act of reconstruction will require more time than making regular entries. And, second, reconstruction defeats the purpose of the log, because, like money, people tend to forget how they use their time shortly after it's spent.

Be honest when keeping the log. If the 10-minute break stretches out to 27 minutes, make a note of it. If the one-hour lunch actually takes 99 minutes, list it. By keeping a time log for a couple of weeks, you'll come to recognize how your time is really being spent.

Many people find that the 80-20 rule applies to them. This "law" states that 20 percent of the known variables produce 80 percent of the results. In the case of self-management, this means that 80 percent of your results come from 20 percent of your activities. Likewise, the other 20 percent of your results come from the remaining 80 percent of your activities. By keeping a time log, you can increase your results by focusing on the productive 20 percent of your activities and taking measures to practice them more often.

- *Maintain a schedule.*

Most people would become much more efficient if they would keep an activity list. Also known as a "to do" list or schedule, it's simply a personal list of errands, commitments, and responsibilities. When one pops into mind, record it on the list. That way, you can keep track of your events without fear of forgetting. Also, an activity list will make you more effective, because you won't be pausing periodically during your day to make sure you can recall all of your obligations.

Each day, review your activity list to determine which events will put you closest to realizing your ambitions. After composing the activity list, prioritize these events. Rank them in order of importance. Then you'll know which activities must be undertaken in which order for best results.

By referring to your activity list often, you can assign "time slots," or specific periods of time, for activities. Some events will be easy to schedule. For example, a 10:00 a.m. appointment with a physician, attorney, or accountant must be scheduled for 10:00 a.m., but obligations such as writing a report or running by the dry cleaners can be scheduled to coincide with your earliest convenience.

Keeping a schedule can help you keep in mind what is important in your life. Again, you only have 24 hours per day. Hopefully, you will be sleeping six to eight of those hours. This means that you actually have 16 to 18 hours of conscious time each day to conduct your activities. Keeping a schedule with an ongoing list of activities will insure the maximum, wise use of your most valuable asset—time.

- *Get organized.*

If you haven't already, it would be wise to organize your environment. This includes your home, car, and work area. Assign a space for all items, and return them to their proper places when not in use. You'll be amazed at the time you save by not having to rummage through clutter. It is also a great psychological boost—a feeling of control and professionalism.

- *Handle papers once.*

When documents and correspondence come to your attention, take action. Don't let them accumulate until you have a monster pile of paperwork to handle. Process papers, and then file or discard them. Don't waste time by shuffling them.

- *Ask for help when you need it.*

It will take you less time to ask for and receive information than to conduct research or, worse yet, to learn by trial and error. Don't be too proud to ask for help when you need it. After all, you'll probably be able to return the favor in due time. This presents a strong case for "mentors," our friends and advisors who have experienced our concerns and challenges.

- *"Add" productive time to your day.*

There are a number of ways this can be done, including waking up earlier, going to bed later, and finding ways to decrease the time devoted to successful completion of your responsibilities. Cut or eliminate breaks and lunch hours when time is of the essence.

- *Allow for emergencies.*

When scheduling activities, don't be averse to overestimating the time required for them. This provides time for emergencies and spontaneous occurrences that require your attention. And if all goes well, the extra time can be applied to a new project or a break.

- *Don't "kill" short periods of time.*

There are so many occasions when we can find ourselves with ten- to twenty-minute blocks of time on our hands. Waiting for meetings and appointments, getting caught in traffic jams, waiting for a bus, taxi, or telephone call all qualify as "dead" time, because most people don't put them to productive use. But these time periods are dead only because we kill them. We think they are insignificant because they're of such short duration.

Do you realize that just 20 minutes a day adds up to more than 120 hours per year? That's three standard work weeks. How many books and magazine articles can you read in 120 hours? How many letters can you write in that period of time? Better yet, how much work can you do? Certainly, some work doesn't lend itself well to such small periods of time. For example, you can't write a report in 20 minutes, but you can certainly outline one. You can't tackle major projects in 20 minutes, but you can brainstorm for ideas for future ones. Keep work, reading material, and basic tools (paper, pencils, and pocket recording devices to make notes to yourself) handy to utilize these brief time periods. Remember, don't be afraid to think big, but don't be afraid to think small, either. By putting these seemingly insignificant periods to productive use, you can achieve significant results over the long haul.

- *Rely on technology.*

    If you're stuck in a traffic jam, you can listen to an instructional CD or something motivational on your iPod. Keep a digital recorder handy to record your thoughts, especially when you can't stop to write them down. Save time with a computer, microwave oven, and dishwasher—whatever helps you add moments to your life.

- *Learn to say no.*

    Not everything you are asked to do will help you realize your goals, nor will an over-abundance of activities always add to a balance between your body, emotions, and spirit. Don't be afraid to turn down requests for your assistance when compliance would interfere with the pursuit of your ambitions. Besides, it's better to refuse a request outright than to commit yourself, only to discover that you don't have enough discretionary time to honor your commitment.

- *Designate a daily private time for yourself.*

Find a period of time, preferably at least thirty minutes to an hour, when you can set up minimal or no interruptions, then claim that time for yourself. Use it to get alone with the Lord, read, pray, dream, and otherwise focus on your most important ambitions. I designate 6:00 to 8:00 a.m. as my special time. A friend of mine reserves the hour from midnight to 1:00 a.m. for his special time, which would be absolutely useless for me to try to do. The main thing is to set your daily private time, then guard that time as sacred. If you don't schedule it and follow through, you won't get it.

- *Do it now!*

W. Clement Stone, best-selling author and positive thinking teacher, popularized this concept, and it's a good one. Don't plan your work to coincide with external deadlines. If a crisis should develop, your project will be in trouble. Set your own deadlines. The more urgency you place on projects, the sooner—and better—they will get done. Also, setting your own deadlines will provide an automatic "extension" should something develop to postpone the project. Procrastination can derail you from the tracks of your ambitions, eating away at your discretionary time. Procrastination also creates "emotional baggage," or guilt over putting things off, that interferes with your effectiveness. If something is worth doing at all, it's worth doing as soon as possible.

- *Discourage interruptions.*

Organize a designated time when you will accept interruptions such as telephone calls, Internet usage, or colleague visits. Keeping your office door closed will cut down on drop-in visitors. Even positioning your desk so you don't face the doorway can discourage interruptions. If people don't make eye contact with you, they'll be less inclined to intrude. You can still be friendly and warm, but you don't have to invite interruptions from everyone who passes your office. Also, avoid interruptions by being careful with telephone calls—handle only the most important calls at once, and return all others during a more convenient single block of time.

- *Respect the time of others.*

The best way to get a reputation as someone who values his or her time is by respecting other people's time. People tend to treat individuals the same way those individuals treat them. If you respect other people's time, chances are good they'll respect yours in return.

These are only fifteen tips. I am sure you can think of many more that can improve your usage of time. Be creative. With these ideas, you can get a good start on managing your time effectively. Together, these elements become powerful tools to help you use your time most effectively as you seek to move successfully toward health, wealth, and wisdom.

A FINAL NOTE

Imagine that a bank credits your account each morning with $86,400. No balance is carried over from day to day. Any balance is deleted each evening. What would you do when you knew that you would not use all your daily balance? You would withdraw every cent, wouldn't you?

You have such a bank, and so do I. The name of our bank is "time." Every day God gives us a bank credit of 86,400 seconds. Every night, that which we have not used is debited from our account. This bank allows no overdrafts, and there is no going back for a second chance on the precious assets that are lost. This bank does not allow borrowing from tomorrow, nor are there leftovers that can be saved for future use. Relentlessly, the clock ticks away, leaving nothing that is unused.

You must invest your most precious asset wisely so you can obtain the best return in terms of health, wealth, and wisdom.

The key is good self-management. Maybe you prefer to use the term "diligence." Certainly, the Bible has plenty to say concerning the benefits of managing your life wisely. Proverbs 10:4 says, *"He who has a slack hand becomes poor, but the hand of the diligent makes rich.* Proverbs 21:5 declares, *The plans of the diligent lead surely to plenty...."*

Remember, long-range ambitions break down to medium-range goals, which break down to short-term ambitions, which are achieved by a workable action plan. Through this process, you can become a master at time-management, which translates into self-management. By maximizing your most valuable asset—your time—you move forcefully toward your goals of health, wealth, and wisdom.

The best way to maintain good self-management principles is to ask yourself periodically, "Is this the most productive use of my time?" If it is, you are in good shape. If it isn't, get back on track. Quickly!

Personal Health, Wealth, and Wisdom Insight

1. Go back and look at the list of time-wasters. What are your top ten?

2. The most important idea I gained from reading this chapter is:

3. My plan for using this time-management idea is:

4. The specific actions I will take to implement this principle are:

5. The results I expect from my usage of this idea are:

Chapter Five Highlights

- Time-management is possible, since it is tied to self-management. By decreasing the time you devote to various obligations, you can effectively increase the amount of discretionary time at your disposal.

- Time-management is nothing more than setting and achieving ultra short-term ambitions.

- Practicing sound self-management principles can help you function effectively in your various life roles as you move toward health, wealth, and wisdom.

- Practice various self-management tips to make the best use of your time.

Allow time for work;
It is the price of success.
Allow time for love;
It is the sacrament of life.
Allow time to play;
It is the secret of youth.
Allow time to read;
It is the foundation of knowledge.

Author Unknown

Chapter Six
Positioning Yourself For Success

Most of us as individuals often act as though we think the future is something that happens to us, rather than as something we create every day. Many people explain their current activities in terms of where they have been rather than in terms of where they are going. Because it is over, the past is unmanageable. Because it has not happened, the future is manageable.

Herbert A. Shepard
American economist

The winningest thoroughbred horses have won millions of dollars, but historically, these champions have won by less than 5 percent in their most important races. That 5 percent has allowed them to win more than 20 percent of the prize money, over their closest competitors.

Five of the closest Boston Marathon finishes have been decided by less than five seconds, yet the difference between first and second place each year, in terms of sponsorship and prize money, is more than 50 percent.

Does this mean that the winning thoroughbreds are

20 percent better or that the championship marathon runners are worth 50 percent more than their nearest competitors? Of course not! But what a difference that tiny differential percentage makes.

As you move toward greater health, wealth, and wisdom, it is important that you understand the fact that you position yourself for success by continuing to get better in all areas of your life, even slightly. That slight-edge advantage can make all the difference in the world, and it can put you in position to achieve far more than those who don't understand this principle.

EXTRA-EDGE POSITIONING

Careers are not determined by wide margins, but are decided by slight advantages. No matter where you work or what you do, as little as a 5 percent extra edge can make the difference between fast-track success and mediocrity.

For that reason, personal and professional positioning has become one of today's important trends.

What is positioning?

- Your positioning power is the way your family, associates, and friends describe who you are and what you do.
- Positioning yourself means doing 5 percent extra, caring a little bit more, going the second mile, doing whatever it takes to succeed.

How do you begin to position yourself well? Let me suggest three foundational strategies:

- *Position yourself a notch above.*

Dress slightly better than required, work more diligently than expected, and learn to be more positive about life than others. You cannot expect others to care about your ambitions if you don't.

- *Position yourself as a person who others can take seriously.*

Suppose your appointment is with a powerful CEO; if you look and act like one of his or her managers or salespeople, you will be treated as an inferior. Position yourself as someone headed for great success. Let your dreams fuel the way you treat others and yourself. You will be surprised at what happens.

- *Position yourself as one who is an effective, powerful communicator.*

Speaking in front of others is one of the greatest fear-factors for nearly everyone. So is writing. While others are held back by these fears, you can walk through the open doors by learning to express yourself effectively.

A professor at the University of California interviewed 10,000 businesspeople over a four-year period on the generic topic, "What causes people to say yes to you?" The professor discovered that the 55 percent who agree with you do so based on your body intensity. Not body language, such as leaning forward or crossing your arms, but whether or not there is a sense of dynamism and believability as you communicate. He also found that 38 percent of those who say yes to you do so because of the quality of your communication, your tone of voice (speaking), or style (writing). So, according to this University of California study, at least 93 percent of our success is based on how well we can communicate. For a salesperson, educator, politician, theologian, or attorney, that may mean that only 7 percent of their success is due to "product knowledge."

Doesn't it make sense that you can position yourself better and make a greater impact, personally and professionally, by mastering basic communication skills? The marketplace is filled with people who may have more technical knowledge, better career paths, or higher IQs than you, but since so many cannot (or will not) communicate effectively, they remain stuck in lower-paying, less-respected positions than those who are better communicators.

Remember the illustrations of Benjamin Franklin, Colonel Harlan Sanders, and Joseph. What made them succeed when most others would have failed? It was many things, of course, but positioning certainly played a major part.

Positioning yourself in the top 5 percent requires a top-flight attitude and singleness of purpose, but it provides that extra edge as you move toward success. The way you position yourself is critical to everything you hope to do or be. Positioning includes the way you dress, think, act, and otherwise identify yourself as someone with something important to say—someone who is going somewhere, someone who can be believed.

In the marketplace, people simply pay more attention to the men and women who have positioned themselves effectively. That slight-edge power brings people and resources your way.

The mega-best-selling author Tom Peters says, "Perception is everything." To a large degree, he is absolutely right. The problem is that most of us are simply not aware of the power of personal and professional perception, which we call positioning.

POSITIONING STEPS

There are many ways, of course, that you can stand out from the crowd as you move toward greater health, wealth, and wisdom. You are unique, so you must seek God's direction as you blaze your own path.

However, there are several basic principles you can use to your advantage, common-sense steps to position yourself effectively. Consider these basics:

- *Present a neat, clean appearance.*

I have already discussed good grooming and hygiene. This is a good time to mention them again.

Be sharp, well-groomed, and reasonably conservative in taste. Ralph Waldo Emerson wrote, "A man's style is his mind's voice." How you look and act are nonverbal messages that speak volumes about the kind of person you are. People notice.

- *Be confident.*

Set a tone of importance. Be yourself, of course, not pompous, but neither should you be so casual or nonchalant that you are perceived as weak or uncaring.

Neither do you have to act superior or inferior. Confidence comes through preparation, courage, and knowing that *"The steps of a good man are ordered by the Lord, and He delights in his way"* (Psalm 37:23). Do whatever it takes to build confidence—even self-talk in front of a mirror. Learn and repeat confidence-building scriptures such as these:

"I can do all things through Christ who strengthens me"
(Philippians 4:13).

"So shall My word be that goes forth from My mouth; It shall not return to Me void, but it shall accomplish what I please, and it shall prosper in the thing for which I sent it" (Isaiah 55:11).

- *Be enthusiastic.*

Remember the story of John Wesley, the eighteenth-century English clergyman and founder of the Methodist Church? At a critical moment in his life, he decided that he wanted to do something different from before. He desired to reach more souls than before. His purpose and mission grew larger than anything that could have held him back. He discovered the power of positioning, and everyone began noticing.

Not everyone appreciated the changes (nor will everyone like the fact that you have decided to position yourself more effectively!). The religious leaders of his denomination gave him the left foot of fellowship, so to speak. Undaunted and even more excited about his newfound purpose, he took his enthusiasm and message to a soapbox in the park.

Soon thousands began coming to hear him preach. Eventually he would become a much-in-demand speaker. During the remainder of his life, he traveled an amazing 250,000 miles on horseback, preached 40,000 sermons, produced 400 books. And at 80 years of age, was ashamed that he could not preach more than twice a day!

Someone asked him once, "How in the world do you do it? You attract so many to hear your sermons, and are converting them by the multitudes."

The clergyman answered, "I simply set John Wesley on fire, and the people come to watch John Wesley burn!"

Positioning, indeed! Be enthused.

- *Smile a lot.*

The single greatest feature you possess, and the one that controls your tone of voice, is your smile. You sound warm and wonderful when you talk and smile at the same time. That smile translates well to the page, over the telephone, and through all forms of business communication.

Comedienne Phyllis Diller once said, "A smile is a curve that sets everything straight." I like what Charles Gordy wrote: "A smile is an inexpensive way to change your looks." The late Mother Teresa said it best: "Every time you smile at someone, it is an action of love, a gift to that person, a beautiful thing."

The Bible says," ...*Happy is that people...whose God is the LORD*" (Psalm 144:15 KJV). Psalm 35:9 declares, "*And my soul shall be joyful in the LORD; it shall rejoice in His salvation.*" Happiness and joy are indications of God's presence in your life. Smiling lets people know that you are happy and filled with joy. Go ahead. People will be attracted to your smile.

Be genuine, of course, and practice in front of a mirror (by yourself!) until you feel confident doing this, but smile.

- *Use a person's name.*

This is a great positioning principle because it seldom is unsuccessful. It has been said that the sweetest sound in all the world to any person is his or her name. People have powerful feelings for a person who makes the extra effort to remember and use their preferred name. It certainly beats, "Hey, you!"

To help remember a name when introduced, repeat the name back to the person: "Mrs. Smith, it is a pleasure meeting you" or "John, you had a great idea on that...." If you have trouble remembering, don't hesitate to ask the person to repeat his or her name. I have yet to see anyone react to such a request in a negative manner.

If speaking to more than one person, attempt to use the names of a few strategic people. When writing, double-check the spelling of names. Names are important. They are the door to a person's heart. When you become proficient at remembering and using names with sincerity, you position yourself a notch above most other people who simply don't understand the importance, don't take the extra effort, or don't care.

- *Don't apologize for taking the other person's time.*

Start your comments on a positive, clear-cut note. End the same way. You position yourself well by knowing your purpose and acting upon it.

- *Be comfortable to be around.*

If you are speaking to an audience of one person or a few, sit down. If a seat is not offered, ask, "Do you mind if I sit?" Translate that same one-on-one feeling when you are writing. You position yourself advantageously when you are comfortable, for you then help the other person to feel at ease.

- *Never stop learning.*

Positioning is often knowing that additional fact, being slightly more informed, having statistics that come from extra effort, as well being able to tap into all that data quickly and effectively. This kind of positioning power comes through a thirst for knowledge. The same information is accessible to everyone, but somehow the top performers in life are able to access that knowledge better than others. You can be one of those extra-edge achievers.

These principles are merely the tip of the proverbial iceberg. You may already be thinking of others that will work well for you. Simply seek to position yourself through everything you say or do. Be genuine as you sell yourself well. Mainly, don't do anything that antagonizes or distracts from what you want to accomplish on your road to health, wealth, and wisdom.

LEVERAGE

One of the best ways to develop a slight-edge advantage as you position yourself effectively is to make the most of your time, talent, and resources through leveraging.

What do I mean?

Archimedes once said, "Give me a lever and I can move the world." He was speaking of a lever made from iron and wood, of course, but he undoubtedly was also referring to the fact that leveraging is most powerful when used with people.

Webster's Dictionary defines *leverage* this way: "the action of a lever or the mechanical advantage gained by it; power, effectiveness" (organizing—to gain greater professional, economic, and political leverage).

Although this definition might seem somewhat abstract in terms of positioning power, it actually is quite focused. You see, the principle of leverage spotlights your power to capitalize on every resource at your disposal.

Without leveraging skills, you simply cannot pursue your goals, because leveraging allows you to tap into resources you never dreamed possible.

EXTRA-EDGE RESOURCES

In 1961, John F. Kennedy announced that the United States would try to beat the USSR in manned flight to the moon. President Kennedy targeted the moon launch, code named Project Apollo, to take place within ten years.

However, there were many elements of a manned flight to the moon that did not exist in 1961: computer technology, scientific knowledge, research and development, manufacturing materials, communication systems, and travel capabilities.

It was a visionary approach, yet JFK immediately asked the Congress and Senate to allocate funds. He established NASA to be responsible for carrying out the details, and he created a framework to make the flight happen.

Very often, when people say, "It can't be done," the truth of the matter may be that they are going to have to do something else to make it doable.

Once you have counted the costs, you must make a conscious decision whether you are willing to commit yourself to that dream and leverage every available resource.

Commitment to your goals does not come cheaply. The bigger the dream, the more expensive it is. However, once you have counted costs and made a definite commitment, you should be able to develop a solid strategy plan. Specifically, you must:

- *Understand the risks.*

There is always an element of risk. In fact, if you take the risk out of life, you take out the opportunity. When you play softball, you cannot get from one base to the next unless you are willing to give up the security of standing on the square bag.

Everyone desires homeostasis or security, but you must also embrace a certain level of risk in order to reach new dreams as you position yourself for greater success. The secret is calculating and controlling the amount of risk as you take the next step.

- *Be willing to forego instant gratification.*

I have found that most dreams ask, "What are you willing to give up to have me?" In effect, to reach higher levels of health, wealth, and wisdom, you need to put aside the American mentality for instant gratification.

Most of us have become accustomed to allocating our resources to present gratifications, as opposed to spending them toward the advancement of our dreams.

This is very closely tied-in with risk. You must risk the instant pleasure of fattening food if your dream is to lose thirty pounds. You may have to risk the present gratification of owning a brand-new Mercedes if your goal is to finish your doctorate.

"But what if I give up these things and still don't reach my goals?" many people ask.

If reaching dreams were easy, everybody would be a successful, well-dressed, satisfied, secure billionaire. Delayed gratification is a key to reaching any big dream, and postponed pleasure helps position you powerfully in today's "gimme-gimme-gimme" world.

• *See the reason for barriers.*

So many people spend all their time lamenting "if onlys" because of a lack of resources or resources that are beyond their reach as they seek to develop leverage. The secret is to get familiar with the resources that are within your reach and keep building on them. This ongoing, consistent application of leverage becomes a habit.

Articles in scientific and business journals tend to depict discovery as a smooth progression, but the actual course is inevitably marked by detours, halts, not enough resources, and other diversions.

Barriers are often the best things that can happen to you, for they force you to refine, refocus, and redirect your energy.

- *Build a network of family, friends, and associates with whom you can share your dreams.*

The late J. Paul Getty, one of the richest men in history, once said, "If you help enough people get what they want, you will automatically get what you want."

Jimmy Johnson was highly successful as a head coach in both college and professional ranks. He was a player on the 1964 Arkansas "Razorbacks" national college championship team, coached the Miami Hurricanes to a NCAA championship in 1987, and then during 1993 added a Super Bowl ring to his jewelry collection as head coach of the National Football League's Dallas Cowboys. He has built a lifetime of peak performance on the principle of leveraging. Of all his championship teams, he says, "The common thread is quality people committed to being the best."

Leveraging means many things. Getting people to work effectively with you is more than a quick-fix—the price is opening yourself to others, trusting them to do a good job, encouraging their growth, and giving them positive reinforcement on a job well done.

If you have not built a network of friends and coworkers—people who rely on you, with whom you can trust vital information, and to whom you can turn in times of crisis—you are missing a key ingredient in the strategy of positioning yourself for success through leveraging resources.

In business, on an athletic field, in politics, and at home, you need a lot of people, spread out in the right places, on whom you can depend (and vice versa). A network is not something that can be established overnight. Your network will require nurturing, but you must develop a strong, supportive group of coworkers and friends.

Just remember: A network is a mutually helpful, flexible group of associates and friends. You cannot build that structure easily. You must be willing to give much more than you get. But by giving unselfishly—giving more than you get—you receive much more than you realize. The good things come back to you and become a vital part of your inner strength.

- *Comprehend God's laws working in your favor as you cultivate resources.*

One the strange things about resources—specifically people, capital, and materials—is that they tend to multiply in direct proportion to the commitment you make: your application. It has been that way throughout history. Bible stories about Abraham, Isaac, Jacob, Joseph, Moses, David, the Lord Jesus, and the apostle Paul bear this out.

When you step out to manage a higher level of performance, that commitment tends to attract more resources. Besides the accounts in the Bible, the pages of history are filled with examples of inventions and advancements that were made en route to other goals. In the midst of great commitment came unexpected resources and solutions. Let me cite a few:

- In 1786, Luigi Galvani noticed the accidental twitching of a frog's leg, and through this research discovered the principle of the electric battery.

- In 1822, the Danish physicist Oersted, at the end of a lecture, happened to put a wire conducting an electric current near a magnet, which led to Faraday's invention of the dynamo (today we call it the electric generator).

- In 1985, Roentgen noticed that cathode rays penetrated black pepper and thereby discovered X-rays, which have been priceless boons to the fields of medicine and industry.

- In 1929, Sir Alexander Fleming noticed that a culture of bacteria had been accidentally contaminated by a mold. He said to himself, "My, that's a funny thing!" He had, through accident, discovered penicillin. Suddenly an entire new door was opened to him, along with greater resources for carrying out his landmark experiments.

- During the 1940s, Percy Spencer and several of his fellow scientists at Raytheon used a radar instrument to cook popcorn and eggs. No one really had an idea what to do with the new technology, so it was 1955 before Tappan built the concept into a home microwave oven, but it did not become a practical, affordable possibility until Amana began making the Radarange® in 1967. This curious oddity has since changed the cooking and eating habits of America. Commitment to an odd assortment of ideas led to a completely new technology.

- In the 1960s and 1970s, 3M® chemist Spencer Silver knew there was something special about his tacky adhesive. He shopped his little vials of glue around the company for five years. The substance was refined by Henry Courtney and Roger Merrill and nurtured to fruition as Post-it® Note Pads by Arthur Fry, who first led singing at his church and used the little slips of paper to mark places in his hymnal.

- The Walkman, brought to life during 1978 by Mitsuro Ida and a group of Sony's electronics engineers in Tokyo, was another accidental product that attracted great resources on its way to widespread use. Originally designed to record and playback stereophonic sounds, it was deemed too large with the complex speakers attached. But the machine became the best-selling electronic device in the world during the late 1970s by removing the speakers and adding one simple modification to the design—lightweight stereo headphones.

You have so many things going for you when you seek to find the right resources for accomplishing something worthwhile. The Law of Reciprocity—what we sow we will reap—only works when you are sowing "seeds" and cultivating "ground."

With great commitment, while positioning yourself for success, you can also experience the Serendipity Effect—being in the right place at the right time so that resources come unexpectedly.

This new insight seldom involves new information. It is almost always a result of a new way of looking at what you already know. Many times, in fact, finding enough resources is just knowing what to do with the resources that are already available to you.

Resources have a way of cascading and multiplying when what you have is already being used, as in the Parable of Talents that our Lord Jesus taught in Matthew 25:14-30.

Time after time, in business and consulting, I have found that as you step out to reach for your dreams, the resources become available.

Earlier in this book, I mentioned the Asian proverb:

"When the student is ready, the teacher will appear." In so many ways, this concept is true. Very few things in life require all of the resources in advance. You must count the costs realistically, of course, but that doesn't mean that you can never do anything until all the resources are in hand.

Can you imagine how many times President Kennedy had someone decry his space program: "Sir, it can't be done because we don't have...".

People who are unwilling to position themselves for greater success say, "There are just too many problems and not enough resources." Those who seek health, wealth, and wisdom reply, "Sure, there are challenges, but let's figure out ways to make it work."

To develop solid strategy plans, you must understand the risks, be willing to forego instant gratification, see the reason for barriers and, comprehend the laws of nature that are working in your favor as you cultivate resources. This will lead you to true riches throughout your life. And it certainly leads to wisdom.

A FINAL WORD

You have so many resources available to you—many, which go completely unrecognized and unnoticed. You have courage, intuition, unseen laws of nature, and unrealized talents. God has placed many treasures inside you that are waiting to be released.

You have a wealth of inner reserves to help insure success every step of the way on your road to health, wealth, and wisdom. The secret is learning to tap into those hidden assets that God has provided.

Sadly, in most areas of life, we often overestimate our poverty by underestimating our resources.

These resources may mean money, knowledge, contacts in the right places, skills, more people—whatever it takes to achieve your dreams and goals. One thing you must know, however, is the greater your ambitions, the more you need to learn how to position yourself for success through the extra-edge advantages, leveraging and developing resources.

Begin to position yourself powerfully. No matter who you are or what you have done in the past, take what you have and use it to full advantage.

Remember, to succeed you need to use your gifts, talents, and skills only 5 percent better than those around you. The results can be astounding!

The difference between a successful person and others is generally not a lack of strength, nor a lack of knowledge, but rather in a slight-edge lack of will. That, in a sentence, is one of the secrets of health, wealth, and wisdom.

Personal Health, Wealth, and Wisdom Insight

1. List three areas of your life in which you are applying the principles of leverage.

2. Write two examples of the resources you are leveraging for each of the above areas.

3. What specific steps should you take to develop better resource-building skills?

4. My best talents, personally and professionally, are:

5. More than anything, I want:

Chapter Six Highlights

- A slight-edge advantage can make all the difference in the world, and it can put you in position to achieve far more than those who don't understand this principle.

- In the marketplace, people simply pay more attention to the men and women who have positioned themselves effectively. That slight-edge power attracts people and resources your way.

- One of the best ways to develop a slight-edge advantage as you position yourself effectively is to make the most of your time, talent, and resources through leveraging.

Resources have a way of cascading and multiplying when what you have is already being used, as in the Parable of Talents, which our Lord Jesus taught in Matthew 25:14-30. Time after time, in business and consulting, I have found that as you step out to reach for your dreams, positioning yourself for success, the resources become available.

History's greatest achievements have been by people who excelled over the masses in their field only slightly.

Louis A. Allen
British-born American essayist

Section 3

Wisdom

Pronunciation: `'wiz-d_m`
Function: *noun*
Etymology: Middle English from Old English w_sd_m from w_s wise

1. **a** : accumulated philosophic or scientific learning : *knowledge* **b** : ability to discern inner qualities and relationships : *insight* **c** : good sense: *judgment* **d** : generally accepted belief
2. : a wise attitude, belief, or course of action
3. : the teachings of the ancient wise men[15]

Chapter Seven
The Beginning of Wisdom

The fear of the Lord is the beginning of wisdom; a good understanding have all those who do His commandments. His praise endures forever

Psalm 111:10

King Solomon, considered one of history's wisest men, was offered a choice. The decision he made changed history:

> "At Gibeon the Lord appeared to Solomon in a dream by night; and God said, "Ask! What shall I give you?" And Solomon said: "You have shown great mercy to Your servant David my father, because he walked before You in truth, in righteousness, and in uprightness of heart with You; You

have continued this great kindness for him, and You have given him a son to sit on his throne, as it is this day. Now, O Lord my God, You have made Your servant king instead of my father David, but I am a little child; I do not know how to go out or come in. And Your servant is in the midst of Your people whom You have chosen, a great people, too numerous to be numbered or counted. Therefore give to Your servant an understanding heart to judge Your people, that I may discern between good and evil. For who is able to judge this great people of Yours?" The speech pleased the Lord, that Solomon had asked this thing. Then God said to him: "Because you have asked this thing, and have not asked long life for yourself, nor have asked riches for yourself, nor have asked the life of your enemies, but have asked for yourself understanding to discern justice, behold, I have done according to your words; see, I have given you a wise and understanding heart, so that there has not been anyone like you before you, nor shall any like you arise after you. And I have also given you what you have not asked: both riches and honor, so that there shall not be anyone like you among the kings all your days. So if you walk in My ways, to keep My statutes and My commandments, as your father David walked, then I will lengthen your days." Then Solomon awoke; and indeed it had been a dream. And he came to Jerusalem and stood before the ark of the covenant of the Lord, offered up burnt offerings, offered peace offerings, and made a feast for all his servants."

1 Kings 3:5-15

Solomon's prayer, asking for wisdom, gave us an exceptional pattern to follow:

- He thanked God for His faithfulness to his father and himself.
- He acknowledged his weaknesses.
- He admitted that God's wisdom alone could govern the nation.

God honored King Solomon's prayer, making him one of Israel's greatest kings, admired far and wide for not only his wisdom but also for the blessing of God that was poured out upon him and his kingdom.

THE ROAD TO WISDOM

Proverbs 4:5-13 tells us that wisdom is the best road to an abundant life:

"Get wisdom! Get understanding! Do not forget, nor turn away from the words of my mouth. Do not forsake her, and she will preserve you; love her, and she will keep you. Wisdom is the principal thing; therefore get wisdom. And in all your getting, get understanding. Exalt her, and she will promote you; she will bring you honor, when you embrace her. She will place on your head an ornament of grace; a crown of glory she will deliver to you." Hear, my son, and receive my sayings, and the years of your life will be many. I have taught you in the way of wisdom; I have led you in right paths. When you walk, your steps will not be hindered, and when you run, you will not stumble. Take firm hold of instruction, do not let go; keep her, for she is your life."

A road or path is a common example throughout the Bible. Wisdom allows us to walk uprightly, so that we will not stumble through the paths of life. Wisdom means hearing and doing God's Word as you walk out your faith. That is why the fear of the Lord is the beginning of all true wisdom.

Where does the road lead? In other words, how do you obtain wisdom? Here are some of the best road signs you will ever see:

• *Understand the fact that true wisdom comes from God.*

First Chronicles 22:11-12 explains: *"Now, my son, may the Lord be with you; and may you prosper, and build the house of the Lord your God, as He has said to you. Only may the Lord give you wisdom and understanding, and give you charge concerning Israel, that you may keep the law of the Lord your God."*

Proverbs 2:6 declares, *"For the Lord gives wisdom; From His mouth come knowledge and understanding."*

Likewise, Daniel 2:23 says, *"I thank You and praise You, O God of my fathers; You have given me wisdom and might, and have now made known to me what we asked of You, for You have made known to us the king's demand."*

• *Ask God for wisdom.*

James 1:5 declares, *"If any of you lacks wisdom, let him ask of God, who gives to all liberally and without reproach, and it will be given to him."*

One of the great truths of the ages is the foundational fact found in James 4:2—*"...You do not have because you do not ask."*

Luke 11:11 tells us that God is eager to give us the

answers to our requests: *"If a son asks for bread from any father among you, will he give him a stone? Or if he asks for a fish, will he give him a serpent instead of a fish?"*

If you want wisdom, ask!

- *Desire wisdom with all of your heart.*

We read in Proverbs 4:8, *"Prize her highly, and she will exalt you; she will honor you if you embrace her"* (RSV). These are not trite or meaningless words. To prize something and to embrace someone implies intense desire and impassioned love. Wisdom must be valuable to you. This is why Solomon wrote, *"...Seek it like silver and search for it as for hidden treasures"* (Proverbs 2:4 RSV).

- Apply yourself to the study and understanding of God's Word.

Psalm 19:7 tells us, *"The law of the Lord is perfect, reviving the soul; the testimony of the Lord is sure, making wise the simple"* (RSV).

The more you devote yourself to God's Holy Word, the more you open yourself up to the greatest wisdom in the universe. Doesn't it make sense, then, to spend more time studying God's Word if you want to pursue wisdom?

As you grow in wisdom, you will become a living example of Proverbs 18:4—*"The words of a man's mouth are deep waters; the fountain of wisdom is a gushing stream"* (Proverbs 18:4 RSV).

- *Obey His Word.*

The Hebrew meaning of *wisdom* includes "separating yourself to God, opening your life to Him, and allowing Him to reveal His road map to you."

Throughout the Scriptures, wisdom and obedience are

used together. Moses, for example, taught us that wisdom consists in knowing and doing the commandments of God. Says Deuteronomy 4:5-6:

> *"Surely I have taught you statutes and judgments, just as the Lord my God commanded me, that you should act according to them in the land which you go to possess. Therefore be careful to observe them; for this is your wisdom and your understanding in the sight of the peoples who will hear all these statutes, and say, "Surely this great nation is a wise and understanding people."*

Christ Jesus essentially said the same thing in Matthew 7:24: *"Therefore whoever hears these sayings of Mine, and does them, I will liken him to a wise man who built his house on the rock."*

Godly wisdom means hearing and doing God's Word. People who obey Him and humble themselves to Him understand the fact that the fear of the Lord is the beginning, wellspring, and unending source of all true wisdom.

WISDOM IN TODAY'S WORLD

How does wisdom relate to people who live right now, rather than during the time that the Old and New Testaments were being written? Let me use the late Dr. Norman Vincent Peale's words: "You can't expect an empty bag to stand up straight."[16]

Wisdom, when founded properly on God's Word, translates well to a world of people looking for those whose lives radiate wisdom. Three major ways you radiate wisdom are:

- *Honesty*

Edward R. Murrow, the pioneer broadcaster, once said, "To be persuasive, we must be believable; to be believable, we must be credible; to be credible, we must be truthful."

This characteristic means to be held in respect, free from deceit. James Kouzes and Barry Posner, in conjunction with professor Warren Schmidt, the American Management Association and the Federal Executive Institute Alumni Association, surveyed thousands of workers, asking them what they considered to be the most important leadership traits in any area of the marketplace. The majority, 83 percent to be exact, expressed belief that a person must be honest before workers were to call a person a leader.

Everything rises and falls with honesty. The rewards for being honest are immeasurable, not just the immediate benefits, but in terms of sustained leadership and long-range productivity.

But remember, honesty isn't measured by degrees—you either have it or you don't. Wise people have it!

- *Integrity*

His core trait, defined as having sound moral principles, goes beyond honesty. Honesty suggests being free of deceit. Integrity suggests doing what is right, no matter what. Though neither trait is passive, integrity seems to be the most active of the two.

Consistency between word and deed is one of the greatest tests with which people judge your integrity. This characteristic is the companion to honesty, and is an absolute necessity if you hope to live a life of wisdom and success.

- *Character*

Character, also called credibility, is who you really are. It is reflected in your "credit rating" with people around you. The person who builds a reputation for excellent character will hold the respect and loyalty of those with whom he or she works, lives, serves, and plays.

Leadership analysts James Kouzes and Barry Posner write:

> *"Credibility is one of the hardest attributes to earn. And it is the most fragile of human qualities. It is earned minute by minute, hour by hour, month by month, year by year. But it can be lost in very short order if not attended to. We are willing to forgive a few minor transgressions, a slip of the tongue, a misspoken word, a careless act. But there comes a time when enough is enough. And when leaders have used up all their credibility, they will find that it is nearly impossible to earn it back."*[17]

Wisdom means everything. It comes from God, and it must radiate outward from deep within, permeating and affecting everything we do.

WISDOM, IN THE END, BRINGS BALANCE AND TRUST

Years ago a farmer owned land along the Atlantic seacoast. He constantly advertised for hired hands. Most people were reluctant to work on farms along the Atlantic. They dreaded the awful storms that raged across the Atlantic, wreaking havoc on the buildings and crops.

As the farmer interviewed applicants for the job, he received a steady stream of refusals. Finally a short, thin man, well past middle age, approached the farmer.

"Are you a good farmhand?" the farmer asked him.

"Well," the man answered, "I can sleep when the wind blows."

Although puzzled by this answer, the farmer, desperate for help, hired the man. The little man worked well around the farm, busy from dawn to dusk, and the farmer felt satisfied with the man's work.

Then one night, the wind howled loudly in from offshore. Jumping out of bed, the farmer grabbed a lantern and rushed next door to the hired hand's sleeping quarters. He shook the little man and yelled, "Get up! A storm is coming! Tie things down before they blow away!"

The little man rolled over in bed and said firmly, "No sir. I told you, I can sleep when the wind blows."

Enraged by the response, the farmer was tempted to fire the man on the spot. Instead, he hurried outside to prepare for the storm. To his amazement, he discovered that all of the haystacks had been covered with tarpaulins. The cows were in the barn, the chickens were in the coops, and the doors were barred. The shutters were tightly secured. Everything was tied down. Nothing could blow away.

The farmer then understood what his hired hand meant, so he returned to his bed to also sleep while the wind blew.

When you are wise—prepared spiritually, mentally, and physically—you have nothing to fear.

How about you? Can you sleep when the wind blows through your life? The hired hand in the story was able to sleep because he had secured the farm against the storm. We as believers in Jesus Christ secure ourselves against the storms of life by grounding ourselves in the wisdom and Word of God. We don't need to understand everything about everything. We just need to hold His hand to have peace in the midst of the storms. That, in the end, is true wisdom!

A FINAL NOTE

In 1923 a group of the world's most successful financiers met at a Chicago hotel. Among those present were these nine men:

- The former president of the largest independent steel company in the world;

- The nation's best-known wheat and commodity speculator;

- The president of the New York Stock Exchange;

- The secretary of the interior of President Harding's Cabinet;

- The president of the Bank of International Settlements;

- The man, known as the "Match King," who headed one of the world's prime monopolies;

- The man who was one of the most successful stock speculators on Wall Street;

- A past chairman of the one of the country's largest utility companies; and

- The former president of the largest gas company in the United States.

Collectively, these tycoons controlled more wealth than existed in the United States Treasury. For years newspapers and magazines had been printing their success stories. The youth of the nation had been challenged to follow the lofty examples of these nine men.

Twenty-five years later, the names remained etched in history, but time had changed everything:

- Charles Schwab, the president of Bethlehem Steel, lived on borrowed money the last five years of his life and died penniless.

- Arthur Cutten, the great wheat speculator, died abroad in poverty.

- Richard Whitney, former president of the New York Stock Exchange, served time in Sing Sing for grand larceny.

- Albert Fall, once a respected member of the President's Cabinet, was pardoned from prison so he could die at home.

- Leon Fraser, president of the Bank of International Settlement, committed suicide.

- Ivar Krueger, the head of the world's greatest monopoly—International Match Corporation—died tragically; as a final irony, whether he was murdered or committed suicide was never established.

- Jesse Livermore, called "the most wondrous of the boy wonders of Wall Street," died by suicide.

- Samuel Insull, once chairman of Commonwealth Edison Company and other utility corporations, was acquitted on embezzlement and mail-fraud charges. He died in Paris in modest surroundings.

- Howard Hopson, the president of the Associated Gas and Electric utility empire, served time in prison for mail-fraud charges and eventually died in a sanitarium.

All of these men had learned how to make money. All were considered to be top leaders. All were feted in the press. All, however, stumbled in the areas of wisdom—honesty, integrity, and character.

But we don't have to judge these men or what motivated them. History has done that for us. Instead, we should learn from their mistakes. Money and possessions are wonderful; however, by themselves, they are a poor substitute for godly wisdom. This is as true today as ever, and it is just as true in a corporate office as it is in the church or in our living rooms.

Begin now by assessing the values that shape the way you treat other people, control your approach toward life, and affect your attitude about your life's purpose. In a very real sense, these are the values that are already impacting your future. Wisdom from God must be at the core.

Possessing wisdom brings rewards, even in this life:
- A good reputation
- Having the confidence and trust of others
- Personal satisfaction
- Peace of mind
- Favor with God and others

There is no price tag for things so valuable, just as there is no price tag for wisdom!

Personal Health, Wealth, and Wisdom Insight

1. Jot down a recent experience in which someone was not completely honest.

2. Write about a recent occasion in which your actions and attitudes were a great example of honesty.

3. What were the results from these two encounters in terms of others' reactions?

4. What were the results from these two experiences in the way you felt about yourself?

Chapter Seven Highlights

- God honored King Solomon's prayer, making him one of Israel's greatest Kings, admired far and wide for not only his wisdom, but also for the blessing of God that was poured out upon him and his kingdom.

- A road or path is a common example throughout the Bible. Wisdom allows us to walk uprightly, so that we will not stumble through the paths of life. Wisdom means hearing and doing God's Word as you walk out your faith. That is why the fear of the Lord is the beginning of all true wisdom.

- We as believers in Jesus Christ secure ourselves against the storms of life by grounding ourselves in the wisdom and Word of God.

Never mistake knowledge for wisdom.
One helps you make a living; the other
helps you make a life.

Sandra Carey

Chapter Eight
How Hungry Are You?

Persons who reach the top rungs in business management, selling, engineering, religious work, writing, acting, and in every other pursuit get there by following conscientiously and continuously a plan for self-development and growth.

David Schwartz, Ph.D.
Best-selling author of
The Magic of Thinking Big

An intriguing story has been passed down through the centuries about Socrates, considered to be one of Greece's best-known philosophers. According to the legend, a young man came to him with an urgent request. "I have walked 1,500 miles from my home to Athens to gain wisdom and learning," the student began. "I want learning, so I came to you. Can you give it to me?"

Socrates reportedly spoke without hesitation: "Come, follow me."

The acclaimed teacher led the student to the seashore.

He walked into the gentle waves until he and his young follower were in water up to their waists. Then Socrates grabbed his youthful companion and pushed his head under the water. In spite of the younger man's frantic struggles, the teacher held him under the surface. After several tense moments, Socrates pulled the young man out of the water, laid the would-be pupil on the shore and returned to the marketplace. When the young man regained his strength, he walked back to Socrates.

"You are a man of learning and wisdom," the young man challenged furiously. "Why did you treat me so badly?"

"When you were under the water," Socrates asked, "what was the one thing you wanted more than anything else?"

"I wanted air!"

Then Socrates said, "When you want wisdom and understanding as badly as you wanted air, you won't have to ask anyone to give it to you. You will get it wherever and whenever you can!"

THIS ONE THING

There was an especially memorable scene in *City Slickers*, the 1991 comedy motion picture starring Billy Crystal. Mitch Robbins, Billy's character, plays a forty-year-old man plagued by a mid-life crisis. He and his friends find renewal and purpose on a cattle-driving vacation.

One of the most memorable scenes involved Mitch as he rode the cattle trail with Curly Washburn, the crusty cowboy played by Jack Palance.

Here is the Cliff Notes® version: Mitch asked for the secret to life. Dramatically, the old man held up his gloved index finger.

"It's one thing, just one thing." Curly went on to say

that if you stick to that one thing, nothing else matters.

Perplexed, the younger cowboy asked, "Do you know what that one thing is?"

Curly muttered, "That's what you gotta find out."

What does the Socrates and City Slicker stories have to do with you? The point is very clear-cut: Until you answer the one-thing question, and unless you get an all-encompassing hunger to see that one thing come to pass in your life, you will not enjoy the dimension of health, wealth, and wisdom that you could enjoy.

Psalm 42:1 shares, *"As the hart panteth after the water brooks, so panteth my soul after thee, O God"* (KJV).

What drives you?

What motivates you?

Is it desperation? Maybe a desire for a better relationship with the Father? Is it overcoming rejection?
What drives you?

My guess—since you are reading a book about health, wealth, and wisdom strategies—is that you want more of those three biggies.

The apostle Paul understood the secret of this one-thing focus that is needed in every area of life. He wrote: *"Brethren, I count not myself to have apprehended: but this one thing I do, forgetting those things which are behind, and reaching forth unto those things which are before, I press toward the mark for the prize of the high calling of the God in Christ Jesus"* (Philippians 3:13-14 KJV).

Matthew 5:6 goes right to the core: *"Blessed are those who hunger and thirst for righteousness, for they shall be filled."*

Your one-thing focus, fueled by your hunger, will propel you to understand and develop a health, wealth, and wisdom ambition that will be revealed through your persistence, self-discipline, ability to overcome defeats and failures, and eventually lead you to make the right kind of choices.

PERSISTENCE

Calvin Coolidge, thirtieth president of the United States (1923-1929), knew about persistence. He graduated from Amherst College with honors, then entered law and politics in Massachusetts. Slowly and methodically, he climbed the political ladder from councilman in Northampton to governor of Massachusetts, then as Warren G. Harding's vice-president, and finally as president of the United States.

Coolidge was "distinguished for character more than for heroic achievement," according to Alfred E. Smith, both a political opponent and admirer. "His great task was to restore the dignity and prestige of the Presidency when it had reached the lowest ebb in our history."

Today Calvin Coolidge is known as much as anything else for the quotation that continues to motivate people all over the world:

> *"Nothing in the world can take the place of persistence. Talent will not; nothing is more common than unsuccessful men with talent. Genius will not; unrewarded genius is almost a proverb. Education will not; the world is full of educated derelicts. Persistence and determination alone are omnipotent. The slogan "press on" has solved and always will solve the problems of the human race."*

Calvin Coolidge's essay on the subject of persistence was a favorite of the late Ray Kroc. It hung on the wall in all of McDonald's executive offices. As Kroc stated in his autobiography, *Grinding It Out*: "We have thousands of success stories in McDonald's and the key element in these individual success stories and of McDonald's itself, is not knack or education, it's determination."[18]

Ray Kroc knew a thing or two about persistence and determination. His story has been told almost as many times as his McDonald's hamburgers have sold around the world.

A milkshake machine salesman named Ray Kroc came upon a popular California business owned and operated by the McDonald brothers. The business sold only 15-cent hamburgers, french fries, soft drinks, and milkshakes. The restaurant offered no dining facilities. Food was prepared for consumption in cars or off the premises, yet demand for the food during lunch and dinner hours was phenomenal.

So Kroc bought franchising rights from the McDonalds and used the Southern California restaurant as a model to help others open up their own McDonald's. Slowly but surely, he built the enterprise into a successful, booming nationwide business. He continued to lead his industry by expanding the McDonald's menu to include larger burgers, other types of sandwiches, several varieties of breakfast foods, salads, ice cream, cookies, and pastries. As traffic increased below the golden arches, buildings expanded to allow indoor dining. Drive-through windows were added for the convenience of the customer who didn't care to leave his or her car.

Has his idea worked?

Certainly!

It is now the biggest restaurant chain in the world. The golden arches are instantly recognizable all over the world. Along the way, Ray Kroc and his amazing business have epitomized persistence as he overcame prejudices, legal action, and competition.

As with the late Ray Kroc, persistence is a conscious decision that you must make every day. It is a choice that must be built on dreams, preparation, and an attitude of achievement. It must become a "one-thing" way of life.

In every man and woman's life, there are times of summit-like challenges—either through defeats or failures. Relatively few people use such tests as opportunities to become stronger and better equipped to meet the challenges of the future. The majority, by far, allow these ordeals of life to annihilate their dreams.

Persistence is one of the most effective keys you can use to overcome these dream-killers.

To attain health, wealth, and wisdom, you must keep going—no matter what. You see, you can have the most grandiose purpose, be empowered to risk and act, fully understand your strengths and weaknesses, but without the discipline to act consistently every day—in spite of failures and defeats—it is virtually impossible to achieve your goals.

SELF-DISCIPLINE

Talent is important, but talent alone will not help you succeed. What you need is a big pot of glue. You smear some on your chair and some on the seat of your pants, you sit down, and you stick with every project until you've done the best you can do.

Persistent performers stay glued to their chairs and postpone pleasure—if they must—so they can reap future dividends. Many non-disciplined people, by contrast, expect instant gratification; then, when rewards don't materialize instantly, they may become frustrated and unhappy.

Fifty years ago, a group of researchers began an ambitious, long-term study of 268 male college students, analyzing the paths their lives were to take. Among these men, now in their late 60s and 70s, the researchers found that school performance was related little to job competence. Qualities such as "steady and dependable" and "practical and organized" ended up being incredibly more important. According to Dr. George E. Vailant of the Dartmouth Medical School, the psychiatrist who now directs the study, one crucial performance trait was what he calls "the capacity to postpone—but not forego—gratification."

To do that, you must endure many defeats and failures, along with the victories and good times.

DEFEATS

Ask Mike Krzyzewski, head basketball coach of the Duke University Blue Devils. I have a special love for ACC basketball, having grown up near "Tobacco Road" and spending fifteen of the best years of my life in the Carolinas. Along with a national television audience, I watched on April 2, 1990, during the final moments, as Coach K knelt in front of his team's bench, obviously wishing that the 102-73 thrashing by the University of Nevada at Las Vegas's Running Rebels were just a terrible dream. But the nightmare was real. It was the most lopsided margin in the tournament's history.

Somehow, Krzyzewski never backed away. He kept imploring his team to play hard, kept applauding the rare good play. When the massacre was over, he refused to offer any excuses.

"They beat us in every way possible," he said to the news cameras afterward, looking squarely into the cameras. "If I had a hat, I would take it off to them."
However, he later related that his thoughts were already racing ahead: "This isn't the end for us. There will be another season, another chance."

Indeed there was. In 1991, Coach K again took his team to the Final Four. Again, the Blue Devils faced an intimidating UNLV team. This time, however, Duke walked away with the championship trophy.

But that wasn't all. The next year, again the Blue Devils powered through the regular seasons and eventually got to snip the championship nets for the second straight time! Throughout the 1990s, they were powerful contenders, going deep in the NCAA tournament each time. Again, in 2001, Coach K led the team to another national championship.

Why would I include a section on defeats in a book about health, wealth, and wisdom? Truth is, I would be remiss to write a book like this without a passage on the realities of shattered hopes. You must be hungry enough to overcome every defeat or the losses will eventually stop you cold!

One of the most important lessons you will learn involves how you respond to defeats. The longer I live, the more I realize that life does not always grant your first dream, or your second, or your fifteenth. Along with your triumphs and successes, you will face obstacles, heartbreaks, tragedies, hindrances, and unavoidable problems.

OVERCOMING CHALLENGES

While most people tend to lose heart and surrender their dreams during life's horrible times, top performers learn these universal principles:

• You must discern the difference between temporary setbacks and permanent losses.

You learned in seventh grade science, "For every action, there is an equal and opposite reaction." If you do anything in life, anything at all, you will encounter opposition. It is a fact.

Still, you cannot turn back every time you run into a wall. It's not always easy to tell the difference between a stepping-stone and a stumbling block, especially when the object seems to be ten feet tall.

Remember these lines from the Kenny Rogers song:

> *"You gotta know when to hold 'em;*
> *Know when to fold 'em;*
> *Know when to walk away,*
> *And know when to run."*

Nobody, but nobody, wins every skirmish or goes through life unscathed. If you cannot conquer every foe, the secret is to decide which victories are worth fighting for, and which are not.

- *Obstacles are there to strengthen you.*

When you misunderstand the purpose of struggles and allow them to breed discouragement, you de-energize the benefits. However, in everyone's life comes those times of overwhelming challenges. Sometimes you have the resources to win. Sometimes every resource you have is tested to the limit. Sometimes you may even be completely overrun.

There will be those times when everything seems unfair. Your faith may be tested, as well as your ability to persist. I have seen some people use these times as opportunities to become better, more seasoned, more faithful people. Most, however, allow these experiences of life to destroy and harden them.

First Corinthians 10:13 tells us, *"No temptation has overtaken you except such as is common to man; but God is faithful, who will not allow you to be tempted beyond what you are able, but with the temptation will also make the way of escape, that you may be able to bear it."*

Dr. Robert Schuller often talks about the challenges on the road of life being stumbling blocks or stepping-stones. The choice is yours.

- *Obstacles offer progressive measurements of your growing strength.*

Challenges give you an opportunity to see how far you have come. When I wrestled in high school, I certainly didn't consider it unreasonable to work up through the ranks; likewise, you should look upon each problem as another chance to measure your inner muscle.

As difficult as it may seem, problems come to make you strong. Heraclitus wrote: "It is not good for all your wishes to be fulfilled. Through sickness you recognize the value of health, through evil the value of good, through hunger satisfaction, through exertion the value of rest."

In fact, one of my favorite columns from Abigail "Dear Abby" Van Buren included this poem:

> *Cripple him, and you have a Sir Walter Scott.*
> *Lock him in a prison cell,*
> *and you have a John Bunyan.*
> *Bury him in the snows of Valley Forge,*
> *and you have a George Washington.*
> *Raise him in abject poverty,*
> *and you have an Abraham Lincoln.*
> *Subject him to bitter religious prejudice,*
> *and you have a Disraeli.*
> *Afflict him with asthma as a child,*
> *and you have a Theodore Roosevelt.*
> *Stab him with rheumatic pains until he can't*
> *sleep without an opiate, and you have a Steinmetz.*

*Put him in a grease pit of a locomotive roundhouse,
and you have a Walter P. Chrysler.
Make him play second fiddle in an obscure South American orchestra, and you have a Toscanini.
At birth, deny her the ability to see, hear,
and speak, and you have a Helen Keller.*[19]

Difficulties actually accelerate your success, especially when you understand the value of opposition. Muscles never got stronger from inaction; much to the contrary, unused brawn tends to atrophy.

- *Failures*

And if defeats aren't bad enough, mistakes can take a toll, as well. Once again, mistakes can be a valuable part of life, for in them we find another reason to keep moving toward our goals, no matter what happens.

The attitude we take toward mistakes and failures separates the successful person from the man or woman who never achieves their God-given potential. The best-laid plans sometimes don't work out perfectly. The pages of history are filled with examples:

Christopher Columbus determined to open a new trade route to India, but he missed it by thousands of miles. Instead, he discovered the "New World." Numerous cities, a country, and even a national holiday commemorate Columbus—not bad for a so-called failure!

Leonardo da Vinci is known primarily as the painter of the mystery lady, "Mona Lisa," and her intriguing smile. Actually, he was the product of a broken home, an illegitimate child who never saw his mother. He was passed around from family member to family member, and eventually lived with his father and sixteen-year-old stepmother. Because of his father's legal profession, Leonardo was considered better than the village children and was never allowed to play with them. His early life was very unsettled, and he never knew what it was to enjoy the fun associated with childhood. Onlookers expected Leonardo to become a dull, sullen boy with antisocial attitudes, but he had an active curiosity. That trait saved him from an otherwise dysfunctional childhood, and he eventually became the leading artist, sculptor, astronomer, aeronautical expert, botanist, engineer, anatomist, author, and illustrator of the fifteenth and sixteenth centuries.

As I mentioned in an earlier chapter, in 1786 Luigi Galvani "accidentally" discovered the principle of the electric battery when through his research he noticed the accidental twitching of a frog's leg—an accident that has changed your world and mine.

Another "accident" relating to electricity occurred in 1822 when Danish physicist Oersted, at the end of a lecture, put a wire conducting an electric current too close to a magnet, which led to Michael Faraday's invention of the dynamo (electric generator).

Henry Ward Beecher, the extraordinary nineteenth-century American minister and author, as a boy was reported to be "a poor writer, a miserable speller, with a thick utterance and a bashful reticence which people took for stolid stupidity."

Booker T. Washington was born a slave, had an early life of extreme poverty and unfair treatment, and yet became one of the most valued educators, authors, and inventors in America's history.

Chemist Paul Ehrlich discovered a drug to treat people who were afflicted with syphilis. It was named "Formula 606" because the first 605 tests had been unsuccessful.

Another man was viewed as a mild lunatic by most railroad executives when he suggested that a train could be stopped by using wind. Yet George Westinghouse persevered and finally sold what is now the Westinghouse Air Brake, which became (and remains) a standard feature on American trains.

Thomas Alva Edison is history's most prodigious inventor and developer of new products, most notably the incandescent light bulb and phonograph. The United States Patent Office granted him 1,098 patents during his lifetime, 122 of them before he was thirty years of age. But he also was known to spend as much as $2 million on one invention that proved of little value. What you may not know is that in 1914, Edison's factory in West Orange, New Jersey, was virtually destroyed by fire. Although the damage exceeded $2 million, the buildings were insured for only $238,000 because they were made of concrete and were thought to be fireproof. Much of Edison's life work went up in smoke and flames that December night. The next morning, Edison looked at the ruins and said, "There is great value in disaster. All our mistakes are burned up. Thank God we can start anew." Three weeks after the fire, Edison managed to deliver the first phonograph.

Henry Ford became the "Father of Mass Production" with his immensely popular automobiles. The Model T, brought out in 1908, had sales of 10,607 the first year. In four years, sales jumped to 168,304, and in four more, to 730,041. During the Model T's lifetime, 1908-1927, production added up to 15,458,781 cars—more than the total of all other cars produced collectively by all other American and foreign automakers during those years. It has been called "the most widely used vehicle in human history." Yet the mistakes Henry Ford made in the development of his cars were many, by his own admissions, including neglecting to put a reverse gear in his first automobile.

In 1929 Sir Alexander Fleming noticed that a culture

of bacteria had been inadvertently contaminated by a mold. Through what seemed like a stupid mistake, he discovered penicillin.

Blind, mute, and deaf from infancy, Helen Keller struggled beyond her immense barriers to learn how to read, speak, and write. Before her death in 1968, at 88 years of age, she became a legendary lecturer, as well as a prolific writer.

Albert Einstein was so slow in learning to talk that his parents thought him abnormal, and his teachers called him a "misfit." His classmates avoided him and seldom invited him to play with them. He failed his first college entrance exam, but a year later he tried again. In time he became one of the world's most famous scientists.

Babe Ruth, after a horrible and disillusioning childhood, set professional baseball's home-run record. Never one to give up, "The Sultan of Swat" also topped the list for strike-outs.

Walt Disney faced scoffing and bankruptcy when he began developing his vision. Today the memory of the man who gave the world Mickey Mouse, Donald Duck, and Disney World stands as a lasting monument to his phrase, "All our dreams can come true, if we have the courage to pursue them."

Margaret Mitchell was motivated to write *Gone With the Wind* after an acquaintance expressed sincere doubt in her ability to write an interesting book. It's still one of the best-selling books of all time, and the motion picture by the same name is considered an all-time classic.

A young Elvis Presley was turned down by a well-known gospel singing group because he "didn't have a very good voice." Undaunted, the young Memphis singer continued. Today it is estimated that Elvis Presley has sold over one billion record units worldwide, more than anyone in record industry history. He appeared in 31 major motion pictures, still seen around the globe in untold languages. Amazingly, except for a handful of movie soundtrack songs, Elvis did not record in other languages, and, except for five shows in three Canadian cities in 1957, he did not perform in concert outside the United States. Still, his recordings and films enjoyed, and continue to enjoy, unparalleled popularity all over the globe, and decades after his death, he is still known throughout the world by his first name.

How different would our world today be if Percy Spencer, along with several of his fellow scientists at Raytheon, had chosen another course of action during the 1940's when they used a "useless" radar instrument to cook popcorn and eggs. At that time no one really had any idea what to do with the new technology. More than a decade passed before Tappan built the concept into a home microwave oven, and it didn't become a practical, affordable possibility until Amana began making the Radarange in 1967. This curious oddity has changed the cooking and eating habits of America.

During the early 1960s, Capitol Records executives passed on an offer to record the Beatles, an up-and-coming group from England. In fact, one expert is reported to have stated flatly, "Groups with guitars are definitely on their way out." Today they still have two out of the top ten selling singles of all time (Elvis also has two), and three out of the top twenty all-time selling albums. Yet no one seems to know what happened to the "groups with guitars" expert.

Today, Post-it Notes are found in ample supply in most office settings. The development of these useful little sticky pieces of paper came about in an interesting way. In the 1960s and 1970s, 3M chemist Spencer Silver knew there was something special about a tacky adhesive he had developed, yet, he never managed to capitalize on his invention. He spent five years attempting to find a marketable use for this special adhesive before he gave up. Later, Henry Courtney and Roger Merrill refined the substance, and it was Arthur Fry who nurtured it, using the little stick slips of paper to mark places in his hymnal as he led the singing at his church. The result: Post-it Note Pads!

The Walkman was another accidental product. Brought to life during 1978 by Mitsuro Ida and a group of Sony's electronics engineers in Tokyo, it was originally designed to record and playback stereophonic sounds. However, it was deemed too large with the complex speakers attached. Later the machine became the best-selling electronic device in the world by simply removing the speakers and adding one simple modification to the design—lightweight stereo headphones. The rest is history.

In 1985, Garth Brooks, buoyed by a regional success, left for Nashville and a career in country music. Rejection after rejection later, he returned back to Oklahoma. He kept performing, honing his skills in honky-tonks, and two years later, he headed back to Music City to try again. He held down a day-job at a boot store, sang on jingles and demos for publishers, and managed to scratch out a meager living. A new manager chipped in the $32.50 entry fee to a Bluebird Café showcase, a performance that led to his first record deal with Capitol and his first album, released in April 1989. The rest, as people say, is history. He now has three of the top thirty best-selling albums of all time, regardless of music style, with sales now nearing 100 million albums. He has won more than sixty major industry awards, including three Country Music Association Entertainer of the Year awards.

You see, some of the most successful people in the

world began their careers among jeers and ridicule. Legion are the ranks of famous artists, authors, actors, entrepreneurs, inventors, musicians, and scientists whose work was initially rejected by critics. But they kept on working and made names for themselves.

Likewise, so many discoveries and breakthroughs seemingly happen by accident. The history of innovation is a long list of failures that eventually led to bigger successes—from the ones I've already mentioned to products such as Pyrex cookware, Jello, Popsicles, Lifesavers, Coca-Cola, Silly Putty, Kleenex, Levi jeans, Band-Aids, Corn Flakes, and thousands more.

When successful people fail, they think about what went wrong and what they can do differently the next time. Frankly, most of us can deal with success, but how we deal with failure is the one thing that determines what we get out of life.

"Good timber does not grow with ease," wrote J. Willard Marriott (Founder of Marriott Hotels); "the stronger the wind, the stronger the trees."

People who fail seem to condemn themselves for every new failure; then slowly back off from giving that total effort until minimal effort becomes the norm. The world is full of people who have quit trying and growing. They wonder why so many others are passing them by as they sit in front of the television night after night.

To paraphrase Ben Franklin: "Most people die at 25. They just aren't buried until they are 75."

People who continually endeavor to reach their goals know that it does not matter how many mistakes they make, or even how many times they fail. What matters is the concentrated attempt to learn from each failure and to improve the next time around. They have purpose and are internally motivated to act, and they act on their purpose day after day—like clockwork.

Being hungry for health, wealth, and wisdom often means understanding that if you try something and do not get the outcome you want, it is simply feedback. Use that information to make better choices about what you need to do to perform at the level you want and to produce the results you desire.

Granted, you may be allowed fewer and fewer mistakes as you move up the success ladder, but you can never reach the point where you stop taking risks.

Make mistakes, but never allow yourself to wallow in your misery. You must be creative, not reactive. Strength only comes through life lessons and character building. Say to yourself, "How can I make this a learning experience and cause something good to come out of this?"

Every problem will change you. There will always be a negative and a positive reaction to a problem. Try to react positively to the problem you have.
Ask yourself:

"What are my options?"

"Which are the best solutions?"

"Which reactions will be negative and which positive?"

"Did I miss God's will in this?"

You see, you can manage your challenges by being determined and hungry. You are not going to be able to control all problems, but you can control your reaction to them. When you control your reaction, you can control the problem's effect on you. That is the bottom line. It is your faith in God, your attitude, your persistence, your creativity, and your perception of things that can get you through the tough times.

A FINAL NOTE

A successful man was asked the secret of his accomplishments. His reply was: "Good judgment."

"Where did you learn good judgment," he was asked.

"From experience."

"And where did you gain your experience?"

"From bad judgment!"

Seriously, I have found that success and barriers are almost always linked. I don't know anyone who has achieved very much without suffering from bad judgment, defeats and failures. In fact, a man or woman who has never been defeated is usually a person who has been ruined.

Earlier I mentioned the movie, *City Slickers* and Curly's "one thing" statement. Later in that same movie is an especially memorable moment that touched many movie-goers. Just before the masterful scene in which the three New Yorkers face the ultimate trail-ride challenge, Billy Crystal's character, Mitch Robbins, seeks to console his pal, Phil Berquist (played by Daniel Stern), who seemingly has lost everything—his wife, his job, possibly even his children.

"I've wasted my life," Phil laments.

"Take a do-over," Mitch urges, "like when we were kids playing a game and things went badly. We'd just start over again. You can do it now. Take a do-over. Your life is a do-over. You've got a clean slate!"

Even though it was merely a scene in a movie, the words spoken by Billy Crystal's character were great advice. No matter where you are in your life, take a do-over. Then be glad for your setbacks. Problems and failures are great do-over points, especially if you want to become a person seeking health, wealth, and wisdom.

Kevin Costner, star of such movies as *Bull Durham, Field of Dreams, Dances with Wolves, Robin Hood,* and *The Bodyguard*, once said:

> *"I made an analogy once of a plane going down and people jettisoning all the weight to keep the plane up. I think one of the first things to go as people's lives start to go down is their dreams. Dreams should be the last thing to go—dreams are things you go down with. If you're left clinging to a piece of driftwood in the middle of the ocean, I'd put on it the word dreams."*

How hungry are you? Will you be persistent and determined to see your goals come to pass? Can your dreams survive? And when you meet defeat or failure, can you get back up, take a do-over, and get started on the road to health, wealth, and wisdom again?

Personal Health, Wealth, and Wisdom Insight

1. What are the worst setbacks you have faced?

2. What did you learn from those "failures?"

3. Do you have the courage to be your own constructive critic? In what ways?

4. Are you improving in the attitude with which you face obstacles? How?

5. What are the best ways you have been able to overcome discouragement?

Chapter Eight Highlights

- Your one-thing focus, fueled by your hunger, will propel you to understand and develop an ambition of health, wealth, and wisdom,

- To attain health, wealth, and wisdom, you must keep going—no matter what. Without the discipline to act consistently every day—in spite of failures and defeats—it is virtually impossible to achieve your goals.

- Life does not always grant your first dream, or your second, or your fifteenth. Along with your triumphs and successes, you will face obstacles, heartbreaks, tragedies, hindrances, and unavoidable problems.

Hang in there! is more than an expression of encouragement to someone experiencing hardship or difficulty; it is sound advice for anyone intent on doing good in the world. Whether by leading or prodding others, or improving oneself, or contributing in the thick of things to some larger cause, perseverance is often crucial to success...Much good that might have been achieved in the world is lost through hesitation, faltering, wavering, vacillating, or just not sticking with it.

William J. Bennett
Best-selling author
The Book of Virtues

Chapter Nine
Living Your Life Right Now

The woods are lovely, dark, and deep,
But I have promises to keep,
And miles to go before I sleep,
And miles to go before I sleep.

Robert Frost
"Stopping By Woods On A Snowy Evening"

One rainy Sunday morning in 1940, a bookish, imaginative fifteen-year-old John Goddard decided to list all the things he wanted to do during his life. He pondered for some time, and then carefully wrote 127 goals on a pad of yellow paper under the title:

JOHN GODDARD'S MASTER DREAM LIST:
RIVERS:
1.   Nile River
2.   Amazon River

3. Congo River
4. Colorado River
5. Yangtze River
6. Niger River
7. Orinoco River, Venezuela
8. Rio Coco, Nicaragua

STUDY PRIMITIVE CULTURES IN:
9. The Congo
10. New Guinea
11. Brazil
12. Borneo
13. The Sudan
14. Australia
15. Kenya
16. The Philippines
17. Tanganyika
18. Ethiopia
19. Nigeria
20. Alaska

CLIMB:
21. Mount Everest
22. Mount Aconcagua, Argentina
23. Mount McKinley
24. Mount Huascaran, Peru
25. Mount Kilimanjaro
26. Mount Ararat, Turkey
27. Mount Kenya
28. Mount Cook, New Zealand
29. Mount Popocatepetl, Mexico
30. The Matterhorn
31. Mount Ranier
32. Mount Fuki

Health, Wealth & Wisdom Strategies for Dynamic Living • 159

33. Mount Vesuvius
34. Mount Bromo, Java
35. Grand Tetons
36. Mount Baldy, California

CAREER/STUDY:
37. Carry out careers in medicine and exploration
38. Visit every country in the world
39. Study Navajo and Hopi Indians
40. Learn to fly a plane
41. Ride horse in Rose Parade

PHOTOGRAPH:
42. Iguacu Falls, Brazil
43. Victoria Falls, Rhodesia
44. Sutherland Falls, New Zealand
45. Yosemite Falls
46. Niagara Falls
47. Retrace travels of Marco Polo and Alexander the Great

EXPLORE UNDERWATER:
48. Coral reefs of Florida
49. Great Barrier Reef, Australia
50. Red Sea
51. Fuji Islands
52. The Bahamas
53. Explore Okefenokee Swamp and the Everglades

VISIT:
54. North and South Poles
55. Great Wall of China
56. Panama and Suez Canals
57. Easter Island

160 • **Beyond the Ordinary**

58. The Galapagos Islands
59. Vatican City
60. The Taj Mahal
61. The Eiffel Tower
62. The Blue Grotto, Capri
63. The Tower of London
64. The Leaning Tower of Pisa
65. The Sacred Well of Chich n-Itza, Mexico
66. Climb Ayers Rock in Australia
67. Follow River Jordan from Sea of Galilee to Dead Sea

SWIM IN:
68. Lake Victoria
69. Lake Superior
70. Lake Tanganyika
71. Lake Titicaca, South America
72. Lake Nicaragua

MISCELLANEOUS:
73. Become an Eagle Scout
74. Dive in a submarine
75. Land on and take off from an aircraft carrier
76. Fly in a blimp, balloon and glider
77. Ride an elephant, camel, ostrich and bronco
78. Skin dive to 40 feet and hold breath two and a half minutes underwater
79. Catch a ten-pound lobster and a ten-inch abalone
80. Play flute and violin
81. Type 50 words a minute
82. Learn water and snow skiing
83. Make a parachute jump
84. Go on a church mission
85. Follow the John Muir trail

Health, Wealth & Wisdom Strategies for Dynamic Living • 161

86. Study native medicines and bring back useful ones
87. Bag camera trophies of elephant, lion, rhino, cheetah, cape buffalo and whale
88. Learn to fence
89. Learn jujitsu
90. Teach a college course
91. Watch a cremation ceremony in Bali
92. Explore the depths of the sea
93. Appear in a Tarzan movie
94. Own a horse, chimpanzee, cheetah, ocelot and coyote
95. Become a ham radio operator
96. Build own telescope
97. Write a book
98. Publish an article in National Geographic Magazine
99. High jump five feet
100. Broad jump 15 feet
101. Run mile in five minutes
102. Weigh 175 pounds stripped
103. Perform 200 sit-ups and 20 pull-ups
104. Learn French, Spanish and Arabic
105. tudy dragon lizards on Komodo Island
106. Visit birthplace of Grandfather Sorenson in Denmark
107. Visit birthplace of Grandfather Goddard in England
108. Ship aboard a freighter as a seaman
109. Read entire Encyclopedia Britannica
110. Read the Bible from cover to cover
111. Read the works of Shakespeare, Plato, Aristotle, Dickens, Thoreau, Rousseau, Hemingway, Twain, Burroughs, Talmage, Tolstoy, Longfellow, Keats, Poe, Bacon, Whittier and Emerson
112. Become familiar with the compositions of Bach,

Beethoven, Debussey, Ibert, Mendelsson, Lalo, Milhaud, Ravel, Rimsky-Korsakov, Respighi, Rachmaninoff, Paganini, Stravinsky, Toch, Tchaikovsky, Verdi
113. Become proficient in the use of a plane, motorcycle, tractor, surfboard, rifle, pistol, canoe, microscope, football, basketball, bow and arrow, lariat and boomerang
114. Compose music
115. Play Clair de Lune on the piano
116. Watch fire-walking ceremony
117. Milk a poisonous snake
118. Light a match with .22 rifle
119. Visit a movie studio
120. Climb Cheops' pyramid
121. Become a member of the Explorers' Club and Adventurers' Club
122. Learn to play polo
123. Travel through the Grand Canyon on foot and by boat
124. Circumnavigate the globe
125. Visit the moon
126. Marry and have children
127. Live to see the 21st century

John's list was adventuresome, to say the least, but doing that was hardly unique. Many people make out life-planning lists. Most of these lists, however, wind up in the trash or with other childhood momentos in scrapbooks. Goddard's, on the other hand, became a blueprint for an incredible journey.

"When I was 15," he told *Life* Magazine's Richard Woodbury, "all the adults I knew seemed to complain, 'Oh, if only I'd done this or that when I was younger.'

They had let life slip by them. I was sure that if I planned for it, I could have a life of excitement and fun and knowledge."[20]

The early accomplishments were the easier ones: learning to type 50 words a minute (#81), becoming an Eagle Scout (#73). But after college, he studied premed and eventually treated illnesses among primitive tribes (#37), and did a hitch in the air force (#40 and #75), he began pursuing his goals in earnest. In the early 1950s, he became the first man to explore the entire length of the Nile by kayak (#1); that celebrated expedition established him as an adventurer-lecturer.

Trim and hardy even after he reached middle age (#102), Goddard continued his quests of climbing, studying, visiting, and exploring. He was nearly buried alive in a Sudanese sandstorm (#13). He was chased by a warthog while photographing Victoria Falls (#43). He saw the Pope at the Vatican (#59). He was bitten by a diamondback rattlesnake during a photo session, while milking the reptile (#117). He went around the globe four times (#124).

Today, as one of the world's famous adventurers and world-class motivational speakers, he lives in California. Articles about him appear in Life Magazine, National Geographic, Reader's Digest, and the book Chicken Soup for the Soul. He has shared these amazing stories with students of all ages all over the world.

And, yes, he still has ambitions. He has reached 109 of his 127 goals![21]

A HIGHER VISION

Throughout the pages of this book, I have shared proven, commonsense guidelines to help you achieve health, wealth, and wisdom. I have attempted to show, through examples and a systematic approach, that ordinary people can become successful in all areas of life—body, soul, and spirit.

In this final chapter, I would like to encourage you to move beyond ordinary. Become extraordinary.

How?

- *Define what success means to you.*

What is your mission? A clear definition will help you keep eventual success in perspective. Fantasyland is a cute place to visit at Disney World, but don't allow yourself to live in a corporate dreamworld. Achieving success does not mean that you leave reality, failure, or problems behind.

- *Focus on today and tomorrow, not your past.*

"Coulda-shoulda-woulda" people are a dime a dozen. They are backward focused. Live your life differently. Be a champion goal-setter. Plan ahead. Set short-, mid- and long-range goals.

American educator Herbert A. Shepard wrote:

> *"Most of us as individuals often act as though we think the future is something that happens to us, rather than as something we create every day. Many people explain their current activities in terms of where they have been rather than in terms of where they are going. Because it is over, the past is unmanageable. Because it has not happened, the future is manageable."*[22]

- *Let your imagination run wild.*

Dream big dreams. Focus on what you CAN do, not on what you cannot. Don't let life pass you by.

John Goddard had a determination to "have a life of

excitement and fun and knowledge." In a single phrase, he wanted to live his dreams. He wanted to live life to the fullest—right now. A higher vision starts with imagination!

Albert Einstein, the brilliant physicist, was fond of saying, "Imagination is more important than knowledge." That's why, if you want to add more meaning and impact to your life, allow yourself a childlike, creative freedom to see beyond the norm.

Wrote L. Frank Baum:

> "Imagination has brought mankind through the Dark Ages to its present state of civilization. Imagination led Columbus to discover America. Imagination led Franklin to discover electricity. Imagination has given us the steam engine, the telephone, the talking-machine, and the automobile—things that had to be dreamed of before they became realities. So I believe that dreams—daydreams, you know, with your eyes wide open and your brain-machinery whizzing—are likely to lead to the betterment of the world. The imaginative child will become the imaginative man or woman most apt to create, to invent, and therefore to foster civilization."

Reaching true health, wealth, and wisdom requires developing an extraordinary, imagination-filled vision of where you are going. When you create a vision for yourself, you become a positive influence. Your behavior and determination becomes a model for others to buy into. That power is a great responsibility.

Robert Schuller, the well-known minister, has written:

> *"Commit yourself to a cause worth living for. Get out of the grandstands and onto the playing fields. Move into the spotlight of creative and constructive involvement. It is the risk-running racer on the track, not the hotdog-eating grandstander who gets the attention, the applause, the encouragement and, finally, the prize. Because the chance-taker is in the spotlight, he attracts support and succeeds. And he wakes up one morning with the really big prize—self-confidence. Remember what has been said earlier—self-love is gained through adventure. Attach yourself to something bigger than yourself. In involvement you will acquire a sense of belonging. By a commitment to people, projects or causes, you will have an opportunity to assume responsibilities. Responsibility generates self-love, for responsibility fulfills the need to be needed."*[23]

Consistently ask yourself, "What if?" Many times, a creative solution can be found simply by setting up imaginary scenarios. Thomas A. Edison asked himself "What if?" on a regular basis—"What if a room could be illuminated by electricity?" "What if sounds could be reproduced from a machine?" "What if there were a device that would project pictures in motion on a screen?"

We don't laugh at the "outrageous" questions anymore because we live in a world where Edison's inventions are commonplace.

Don't be afraid to ask your own "What ifs?" Who knows what new solutions you may create.

- *Treat failure and success as the same.*

Every life has both victories and losses. Stand apart from both and examine why each occurred to you. Remember, no matter what—tomorrow is a new day! You can take do-overs. That fact, in itself, is a vital dimension of your performance management spiral.

- *Refuse to live a monotonous life.*

People who follow a routine day in and day out often get bored with life itself, and why not? With an average life span of seventy-plus years, it seems like such a waste for people to spend five to seven days per week, each week of their lives, doing the same thing.

Variety is not only the spice of life, but it's also a good way to open your mind to new possibilities. Don't be afraid to do different things. Take a walk during lunch. Find a new route to work. Don't keep your radio dial stuck on the same station. Buy an iPod, even if you don't know how to use it. Try something new for dinner. If you like rock music, attend a symphony. If you're a classical music buff, check out a rock concert. Learn to play a music instrument, no matter what your age. Develop new friendships. Subscribe to a different magazine or newspaper. The world is full of ideas, but you must be exposed to them to get the benefit. After all, consider what might have happened if Ray Kroc had never discovered the McDonald brothers!

- *Adapt, don't just adopt.*

Ray Kroc adapted the McDonald brothers' marketing plan geared for a relatively small town and made it work from coast-to-coast. That's adaptation, not adoption.

Good musicians don't copy other musicians' arrangements; they adapt them to suit their own tastes and styles—

that is what makes for originals such as Louis Armstrong, Elvis Presley, B.B. King, the Beatles, dc Talk, and so many more.

Whatever part of the marketplace you occupy, don't be afraid to take other people's ideas and apply them to your own needs. Then develop something unique.

- *Don't impose man-made limitations on yourself.*

You have God-given skills and talents. Use His standards for the way you think, not just those of people around you. Worse, don't always accept, "That's the way it's always been done."

- *Seek creative role models, mentors, and friends.*

When desiring to develop a certain behavior, it's good to have role models and friends who practice that behavior. Likewise, if you desire to live creatively, it's a good idea to associate with creative, extraordinary people.

- *Know where you are going.*

Through the years, I have done quite a bit of television production all over the world for Dr. Billy Graham. I have seen him in numerous situations—huge crowds, small gatherings, and one-on-one situations. Believe me, he filled up a room. He had greatness and an anointing all over him. And he was always a perfect gentleman to everyone he met. Few situations, however, were as heartwarming and touching as the time in January 2000 when he spoke at a luncheon in his honor before a number of leaders in Charlotte, North Carolina.

Dr. Graham initially hesitated to accept the invitation because he was struggling with the Parkinson's disease that has afflicted his earthly body for years.

But the Charlotte leaders wanted to honor their native

son. They didn't expect a major address. They just wanted to celebrate his life. Finally he agreed.

After wonderful things were said about him, Dr. Graham stepped to the rostrum, looked at the crowd, and said, "I'm reminded today of Albert Einstein, the great physicist who this month has been honored by *Time* Magazine as the 'Man of the Century.' Einstein was once traveling from Princeton on a train when the conductor came down the aisle, punching the tickets of every passenger. When he came to Einstein, Einstein reached in his vest pocket. He couldn't find his ticket, so he reached in his trouser pockets. It wasn't there, so he looked in his briefcase but couldn't find it. Then he looked in the seat beside him. He still couldn't find it.

"The conductor said, 'Dr. Einstein, I know who you are. We all know who you are. I'm sure you bought a ticket. Don't worry about it.'

"Einstein nodded appreciatively. The conductor continued down the aisle punching tickets. As he was ready to move to the next car, he turned around and saw the great physicist down on his hands and knees looking under his seat for his ticket.

"The conductor rushed back and said, 'Dr. Einstein, Dr. Einstein, don't worry, I know who you are. No problem. You don't need a ticket. I'm sure you bought one.'
"Einstein looked at him and said, 'Young man, I too, know who I am. What I don't know is where I'm going.'"

Having said that, Billy Graham continued, "See the suit I'm wearing? It's a brand-new suit. My wife, my children, and my grandchildren are telling me I've gotten a little slovenly in my old age. I used to be a bit more fastidious. So I went out and bought a new suit for this luncheon and one more occasion. You know what that occasion is? This is the suit in which I'll be buried. But when you hear I'm dead, I don't want you to immediately remember the suit I'm wearing. I want you to remember this: I not only know who I am—I also know where I'm going."

A FINAL NOTE

An extraordinary life of health, wealth, and wisdom is no accident. The steps you have learned throughout this book can make a major positive difference in every area of your life, but you must master the concepts as you allow God to direct your steps. Let this process empower you toward a life of adventure.

Today is the best time to live, not tomorrow, and certainly not some more convenient time in the distant future. Today is when your best dreams can be dreamed and your best work can be done. Right now is when we plant ourselves in the present for the great harvest. Today is seed time. Now is when you work toward the future.

Jeremiah 31:17 declares, *"There is hope in your future, says the Lord..."* The successful future He has designed for you is an ongoing process that takes work, patience, and focus. This is why so few people ever achieve the health, wealth, and wisdom that God has planned for them. That is also the reason why the rewards—for those who do—are bountiful.

Your options are as bright as you want them to be, so live your life to the fullest—right now!

Personal Health, Wealth, and Wisdom Insight

1. Go back and read John Goddard's Master Dream List at the beginning of this chapter. While I don't encourage you to copy his ideas directly, let his ideas inspire you to spend time listing at least twenty of the things you would like to do, study, see, visit, and experience during the remainder of your life.

2. What are the top five things that you want to do first? Why?

Chapter Nine Highlights

- Develop a higher vision, a game plan for an extraordinary life of health, wealth, and wisdom.

- Above all else, know who you are and where you are going!

Be assured, it's not possible for human beings to be empty vessels. No person who has ever lived has been an unbeliever, despite what they may argue. Everyone believes in something. It might be God or not God, manifest greed for money or power, a career or a friend, science, a principle—something. Whatever it is we place before ourselves is what we run toward[24]

Walter Anderson

A Final Word

Pain is temporary. It may last a minute, or an hour, or a day, or a year, but eventually it will subside and something else will take its place. If I quit, however, it lasts forever.

Lance Armstrong
*considered to be the
greatest cyclist in history*

You will face challenges on your road to health, wealth, and wisdom. I know because my own life, in my own way, has been a series of accidents, failures, and successes that I have worked through and tried to make the best of. One of the most valuable things I have learned is the ability to face the day—today—no matter what happened yesterday.

Lance Armstrong continues to live an extraordinary life. Even as a boy, he could ride a bicycle like the wind. At age thirteen, he won a triathlon. At sixteen he became a professional cyclist and began a string of amazing victories—stage victories in the Tour de France, multiple wins in the Tour du Pont, and a slot on the United States Olympic team. During 1996 he reached the apex, named the top ranked cyclist in the entire world.

Then unspeakable tragedy struck. First came the report of testicular cancer. Then came the additional, crushing news. Cancer spread to his lungs and brain. Doctors gave him less than a 50 percent chance of recovery and started a chemotherapy treatment.

Even during the darkest days, Lance spoke of cycling again. Doubtless, those around him hoped and prayed that he was right. Still...

The prayers of people all over the world worked. The therapy worked. Armstrong was quoted as saying that the cancer was "the best thing that ever happened to me." And by 1999, he entered the Tour de France, considered the most grueling cycling event in the world. He amazed the world, not only by finishing but winning. More astonishingly, in what must undoubtedly be one of the greatest achievements in modern sports history, he continued winning the celebrated race.

Who will ever forget that day in Paris as one last time, "The Star-Spangled Banner" rang out over the Champs-Elysees in honor of Lance Armstrong? One last time, on the podium against the backdrop of the Arc de Triomphe, the cancer survivor who became the greatest cyclist in Tour de France history slipped into the leader's yellow jersey. This time, it was the winner's jersey, for an unprecedented seventh consecutive year in the world's most grueling race.

FUTURE VIEW

As Lance Armstrong's life has proven, challenges are simply opportunities dressed in working clothes. J. L. Allen said it this way:

> *"It's the defeat more than anything else that hurts you! Defeat is always the hardest thing for you to stand, even in trifles. But don't you know that we have to be defeated in order to succeed? Most of us spend half our lives fighting for things that would only destroy us if we got them. A man who has never been defeated is usually a man who has been ruined.*

For most people, life is lived between watershed events and problems, and we become more effective and learn more about who we are when we have challenges with which to deal. Those trials prepare us for greater success in the future.

Perhaps the late Jackie Kennedy Onassis, wife of our thirty-fifth president, said it best:

> *"I have been through a lot and I have suffered a great deal. But I have had lots of happy moments as well. I have come to the conclusion that we must give to life at least as much as we receive from it. Every moment one lives is different from the other. The good, the bad, hardship, the joy, the tragedy, love and happiness are all interwoven into one single indescribable whole that is called LIFE. You cannot separate the good from the bad. And, perhaps, there is no need to do so either."*[25]

There will be both tragedies and victories throughout your life. The question is how well will you deal with them. It is this point, perhaps above all, that will help propel you on your search for health, wealth, and wisdom.

You are on a journey, but so many people enter the future backwards, eyes cast longingly on the things that might have been. They don't see where they are going. Their gaze is riveted on the places from which they have come. That is a sure prescription for failure.

No wonder a 73-year-old Thomas Jefferson, third U.S. president, wrote in a 1816 letter to John Adams, his predecessor, *"I like the dreams of the future better than the history of the past."*

It is important for you to turn around and see exactly where you are going. The future is full of main roads, scenic superhighways, pleasant trails, and turnpikes. Seek God's guidance, and then pick your route. Select your rate of travel. Don't quit. The future is up to you!

A FINAL, FINAL NOTE

I have said it before, but I'll say it again: Your options are as bright as you want them to be. God obviously desires to bless you. He designed you. He even sent His Son to live and die on this earth as a sacrifice for your life. He loves you with an unthinkable, supernatural love.

John 15:9 offers an enduring glimpse into the love Jesus Christ died to offer you: *"As the Father loved Me, I also have loved you; abide in My love."*

God-given dreams inside you are waiting to be unleashed. Where these ambitions take you depends upon the choices you make. May your journey always look forward and upward!

I challenge you to recognize and grasp your God-given talents and to utilize the principles you have learned to move your life forward in an exciting experience.

Turn your dreams into health, wealth, and wisdom, for according to 3 John 2, *"Beloved, I pray that you may prosper in all things and be in health, just as your soul prospers."* And Proverbs 15:24 tells us, *"The way of life winds upward for the wise...."*

Now, what will you do with the promises God has given?

> *"But you, beloved, building yourselves up on your most holy faith, praying in the Holy Spirit, keep yourselves in the love of God, looking for the mercy of our Lord Jesus Christ unto eternal life... Now to Him who is able to keep you from stumbling, and to present you faultless before the*

presence of His glory with exceeding joy, to God our Savior, Who alone is wise, be glory and majesty, dominion and power, both now and forever. Amen."

Jude 1:20-21; 24-25

End Notes

1. Merriam-Webster Online Dictionary, Copyright © 2006 by Merriam-Webster, Incorporated

2. Dake, Finis Jennings, Dake's Annotated Reference Bible (Lawrenceville, GA: 1984), 41

3. Ibid, 45.

4. Emerson, Ralph Waldo, *Self-Reliance*, 215.

5. Dychtwald, Ken, *Bodymind* (Los Angeles: J. P. Tarcher, 1986), 131.

6. NOTE: "Charles" is based on an actual story, but the name and certain identifying details have been changed to honor his privacy. Likewise, most of the personal illustrations throughout this book have been similarly changed or otherwise edited to provide anonymity, unless otherwise noted.

7. Harman, Willis, Ph.D., *Global Mind Change* (Sausalito, CA: Institute of Noetic Sciences, 1988), 164-7.

8. Peck, M. Scott, *The Road Less Traveled* (New York: Simon & Schuster, 1978), 42.

9. Bruch, Dr. Hilde, *Learning Psychotherapy* (Cambridge, MA: Harvard University Press, 1974), ix.

10. Peck, 43-4.

11. Mundell, E.J., *"Got Gum Trouble? Your Heart Might Be Next,"* HealthDay News (www.healthdaynews.com), November 29, 2005.

12. Merriam-Webster Online Dictionary copyright © 2006 by Merriam-Webster, Incorporated.

13. Capps, Charles, *The Tongue—A Creative Force* (Tulsa, OK: Harrison House, 1976), 10.

14. Helmstetter, Shad, Ph.D., *What to Say When You Talk to Your Self* (New York: Simon & Schuster/Pocket Books, 1986), 20.

15. Merriam-Webster Online Dictionary, Copyright © 2006 by Merriam-Webster, Incorporated.

16. Blanchard, Kenneth and Peale, Norman Vincent, *The Power of Ethical Management* (New York: William Morrow, 1988), 42.

17. Kouzws, James M. and Posner, Barry Z., *The Leadership Challenge* (San Francisco: Jossey-Bass Publishers, 1987), 42.

18. Kroc, Ray, *Grinding It Out* (New York: St. Martin's Press, 1987), 57.

19. Van Buren, Abigail, *Quotable Quotations*, compiled by Lloyd Cory (Wheaton, Ill: Victor Books, 1985), 427.

20. Woodbury, Richard, *"One Man's Life of No Regrets," Life*, March 24, 1972.

21. For more information about John Goddard, contact Premiere Speakers Bureau, 1000 Corporate Centre Drive Ste. 120, Franklin, TN 37067 (615) 261-4000, or www.premierespeakers.com

22. 22. Brill, Peter, M.D., and Hayes, John P., *Taming Your Turmoil* (Englewood Cliffs, NJ: Prentice-Hall, 1981), 69.

23. Schuller, Robert H., *Self-Love: The Dynamic Force of Success* (New York: Hawthorn Books, 1969), 134.

24. Anderson, Walter, *The Greatest Risk of All* (Boston: Houghton Mifflin Company, 1988), 238.

25. Heymann, C. David, *A Woman Named Jackie* (New York: Lyle Stuart Books, 1989), 558.